Updated 2024

Egyptian Cosmology

The Animated Universe

Expanded Third Edition

Moustafa Gadalla

**Egyptian Cosmology
The Animated Universe
Expanded Third Edition**
by Moustafa Gadalla

CONTENTS

PART II : THE PRINCIPLES AND PRINCIPALS OF
CREATION

1

ABOUT THE AUTHOR

Moustafa Gadalla is an Egyptian-American independent Egyp-tologist who was born in Cairo, Egypt in 1944. He holds a Bache-lor of Science degree in civil engineering from Cairo University.

From his early childhood, Gadalla pursued his Ancient Egyptian roots with passion, through continuous study and research. Since 1990, he has dedicated and concentrated all his time to researching and writing.

Gadalla is the author of twenty-two published internationally acclaimed books about the various aspects of the Ancient Egypt-ian history and civilization and its influences worldwide. In addition he operates a multimedia resource center for accurate, educative studies of Ancient Egypt, presented in an engaging, practical, and interesting manner that appeals to the general pub-lic.

He was the Founder of Tehuti Research Foundation which was later incorporated into the multi-lingual Egyptian Wisdom Center (https://www.egyptianwisdomcenter.org) in more than ten languages.The website also includes another ongoing activity; his creation and production of performing arts projects such as the Isis Rises Operetta, Horus The Initiate Operetta; Egyptian Goddesses Operetta; and a few more other productions to follow.

2

PREFACE [2ND EDITION]

Almost all Egyptologists interpreted, and continue to interpret, the Ancient Egyptian writings and other modes of expression (art, architecture, etc.) without trying to understand the thoughts and beliefs expressed in them. Their explanations continue to be shallow, which reflects their pre-conceived notions of the Ancient Egyptians as being primitive and inferior to the modern Western world.

About a half-century ago, Alexandre Piankoff summed up the deteriorated status of Egyptology in the following statements from his book, *The Tomb of Ramses VI*, 1954:

> *For the early Egyptologists this religion was highly mysterious and mystical. They saw it with eyes of a Father Kircher. Then came a sudden reaction: scholars lost all interest in the religion as such and viewed the religious texts merely as source material for their philological-historical research.*
>
> *Under the sway of Higher Criticism, the texts were decomposed and their genesis eagerly studied...The intrinsic value of religious composition and thought was systematically ignored and consequently temporarily lost. Egyptian scholars since Champollion saw in the oldest religious lore of humanity*

mainly a collection of distorted historical data out of which he endeavored all his life to reconstruct the history of ancient Egypt.

It is time to undo the distortion.

Moustafa Gadalla

2001

3

PREFACE [3RD EDITION]

This book being the Third Edition is a revised and expanded edition of the Second Edition of *Egyptian Cosmology: The Animated Universe*, published in 2001.

The First Edition [1997] was originally published as *Egyptian Cosmology: The Absolute Harmony*, and was changed to better reflect the expanded content of the book.

This book surveys the applicability of Egyptian cosmological concepts to our modern understanding of the nature of the universe, creation, science, and philosophy. Egyptian cosmology is humanistic, coherent, comprehensive, consistent, logical, analytical, and rational. The reader will discover the Egyptian concept of the universal energy matrix, how the social and political structures were a reflection of the universe, the interactions between the nine universal realms, etc.

It is the aim of this book to provide such an exposition; one which, while based on sound scholarship, will present the issues in language comprehensible to non specialist readers. Technical terms have been kept to a minimum. These are explained, as non technically as possible, in the glossary. This Expanded Version of the book is divided into five parts containing a total of 21 chapters.

Part I: The Egyptian Mystical Monotheism consists of one chapter:

Chapter 1: *The Most Religious* will cover the deep mystical meaning of monotheism for the deeply religious Egyptians as well as providing an overview of their cosmic consciousness.

Part II: The Principles and Principals of Creation consists of three chapters—2 through 4:

Chapter 2: *The Animating Energies of The Universe* will cover the scientific understanding by the Egyptians of the state of the world prior to creation and the animating divine energies of the creation cycle.

Chapter 3: *The Pictorial Metaphysical Images* will cover the scientific basis for the Egyptians' pictorial symbolism of metaphysical concepts and the process by which the Egyptian ideographs were manifested in such figurations.

Chapter 4: *The Egyptian Creation Process Accounts* will cover an overview of the three primary phases of the Creation Cycle.

Part III: The Creation Numerical Codes has ten chapters—chapters 5 through 14:

Chapter 5: *Numerology of the Creation Process* will cover number mysticism in Ancient Egypt, and provides analysis of the numbers two, three and five

Chapter 6: *The Dualistic Nature* will cover the dualistic nature of creation and analysis of 14 various applications in the Ancient Egyptian system.

Chapter 7: *Three—Trinities* will cover this first odd number [one is not a number], the significance of the triple powers of a trinity in the universe and a few applications of such principle in the Ancient Egyptian system.

Chapters 8 throughout 14 will cover the **mystical aspects of numbers four through ten.**

Part IV: As Above So Below has five chapters—15 through 19:

Chapter 15: ***The Human Being—The Universal Replica*** will cover how the physical and metaphysical components of man are an image of the whole creation.

Chapter 16: ***Social & Political System*** will show how the social/political structure in Ancient Egypt is a reflection of cosmic principles

Chapter 17: ***The Cosmic Link*** will cover the role of the pharaoh as the cosmic link for the Ancient Egyptians and his demise if he does not serve his functions.

Chapter 18: ***The Physical/Metaphysical Society*** will cover the various modes of maintain communications between earthly living beings and other realms of the universe.

Chapter 19: ***Astronomical Consciousness*** will cover the advanced knowledge of astronomy and time keeping in Ancient Egypt and the zodiac and Sothic cycles; as well as the nature of the harmony of the (seven) spheres and the populace's participation in their maintenance.

Part V: From Mortals To Immortals has two chapters—20 and 21:

Chapter 20: ***Our Earthly Voyage*** will cover the available ways an individual can achieve reunion with the Divine Source, including Sufism, Alchemy, etc.

Chapter 21: ***Climbing The Heavenly Ladder*** will cover life

after earth, soul transmigration, progression along the various realms towards reunification and deitification.

Moustafa Gadalla

4

STANDARDS AND TERMINOLOGY

1 – The Ancient Egyptian word, neter, and its feminine form netert, have been wrongly, and possibly intentionally, translated to 'god' and 'goddess' by almost all academicians. Neteru (plural of neter/netert) are the divine principles and functions of the One Supreme God.

2 – You may find variations in writing the same Ancient Egyptian term, such as Amen/Amon/Amun or Pir/Per. This is because the vowels you see in translated Egyptian texts are only approximations of sounds which are used by Western Egyptologists to help them pronounce the Ancient Egyptian terms/words.

3 – We will be using the most commonly recognized words for the English-speaking people that identify a neter/netert [god, godess] or a pharaoh or a city; followed by other 'variations' of such a word/term.

It should be noted that the real names of the deities (gods, goddesses) were kept secret so as to guard the cosmic power of the deity. The Neteru were referred to by epithets that describe particular qualities, attributes and/or aspect(s) of their roles. Such applies to all common terms such as Isis, Osiris, Amun, Re, Horus,etc

4 – When using the Latin calendar, we will use the following terms:

BCE – Before Common Era. Also noted in other references as BC.

CE – Common Era. Also noted in other references as AD.

5 – The term Baladi will be used throughout this book to denote the present silent majority of Egyptians that adhere to the Ancient Egyptian traditions, with a thin exterior layer of Islam.[See *Ancient Egyptian Culture Revealed,* by Moustafa Gadalla, for detailed information.]

6 – There were/are no Ancient Egyptian writings/texts that were categorized by the Egyptians themselves as "religious", "funerary", "sacred", etc. Western academia gave the Ancient Egyptian texts arbitrary names, such as the "Book of This" and the "Book of That", "divisions", "utterances", "spells", etc. Western academia even decided that a certain "Book" had a "Theban version" or "this or that time period version". After believing their own inventive creation, academia accused the Ancient Egyptians of making mistakes and missing portions of their writings (?!!).

For ease of reference, we will mention the common but arbitrary Western academic categorization of Ancient Egyptian texts, even though the Ancient Egyptians themselves never did.

5

MAP OF ANCIENT EGYPT

PART I : THE EGYPTIAN MYSTICAL MONOTHEISM

Chapter 1 : The Most Religious

1.1 THE EGYPTIANS' COSMIC CONSCIOUSNESS

The Greek historian Herodotus (500 BCE) stated:

> *"Of all the nations of the world, the Egyptians are the happiest, healthiest and most religious".*

The excellent condition of the Egyptians was attributed to their application of metaphysical realities in their daily life—in other words, total cosmic consciousness.

The scenes of daily activities depicted on the walls inside Egyptian tombs show a strong perpetual correlation between the earth and heavens. The scenes provide graphical representation of all manner of activities: hunting, fishing, agriculture, law courts, and all kinds of arts and crafts. Portraying these daily activities in the presence of the neteru (gods, goddesses) or with their assistance signifies their cosmic correspondence.

The most religious Ancient Egyptian never, either in the hundreds of found papyri or other writing surfaces, refers to a human being as a "discoverer' or as an "inventor." The Divine is and was the source of all their existence. The Divine is the origin of all that exists, and it is through the Divine Forces that the universe was created and is being maintained. It is therefore that all aspects of knowledge in Ancient Egypt are credited to the attributes/aspects/qualities of the Divine—namely, the neteru (gods/goddesses).

This perpetual correlation—cosmic consciousness—was echoed in Asclepius III (25) of the Hermetic Texts:

> *"...in Egypt all the operations of the powers which rule and work in heaven have been transferred to earth below...it should rather be said that the whole cosmos dwells in [Egypt] as in its sanctuary..."*

Every action, no matter how mundane, was in some sense a cosmic correspondence act: plowing, sowing, reaping, brewing, the sizing of a beer mug, building ships, waging wars, playing games—all were viewed as earthly symbols for divine activities.

In Egypt, what we now call religion was so widely acknowledged that it did not even need a name. For them, there was no perceived difference between sacred and mundane. All their knowledge that was based on cosmic consciousness was embedded into their daily practices, which became traditions.

Foreign visitors to Egypt who are unfamiliar with the cosmic depth of the natives' traditions are unwise to hastily label the Ancient and Baladi Egyptians as "superstitious."

We do many things in life, such as operating a computer, without most of us knowing how they work. This does not invalidate our computer use as being unscientific. Likewise, the Ancient and Baladi Egyptians' practices should not be dismissed because not everyone knows the scientific basis for that perpetual cosmic action.

In any society, only a relatively few specialized people know the scientific basis for how/why things work in certain ways.

1.2 THE UNITY OF MULTIPLICITY OF THE UNIVERSE

The word 'cosmology' means the study of the universe as a whole and of its form, nature, and physical system.

We find the essence of the word 'cosmology' in the Ancient Egyptian *Litany of Re,* where Re—the Divine Principle of Creation—is described as:

"The One Joined Together,
Who Comes Out of His Own Members".

The Ancient Egyptian definition of Re is the perfect representation of the Unity that comprises the putting together of the many diverse entities, i.e. The One Who is the All.

The *Litany of Re* describes the aspects of the creative principle: being recognized as the neteru (gods, goddesses) whose actions and interactions in turn created the universe.

Let us look at the word 'religion' which had its original meaning twisted.

The root of the word religion is 'religio', which means *to bind or tie together,* which again is consistent with the definition of Re in the Egyptian texts.

1.3 AMEN-RENEF: THE UNDEFINED

The deeply religious Egyptians, recognizing that no human being can define the indefinable, believed in the presence of an unlimited and unknowable power that is too majestic to communicate with the created universe; but without this power, no creation can exist.

Outside the universe and its cyclical nature is what the Ancient Egyptians referred to as 'Amen-Renef', which is not a name of any entity, but a sentence that means *That with Unknown Essence.* In this realm of the unknowable, no words in terms of human thought could be spoken, and the deeply religious Egyptians never did, so they could only be conveyed by negation of all qualities. The Egyptians would say:

– Whose name is unknown to all neteru (gods, goddesses)
– Who has no definition, [i.e. cannot be defined/described in any human term]
– Who has no image.
– Who has no form.
– Who has no beginning and no end; etc., etc.

As such, the Ancient Egyptian *expression* Amen-Renef transcends even the quality of being. Amen-Renef is not the Creator or the First-Cause. All the terms: God, Creator, Master of the Universe, First Cause, The First, are lower principles and separate from Amen-Renef.

The Egyptians uttered no more of it—and then only under infinite reserve, appealing always to a deep sense behind the words: that Amen-Renef is everywhere in the sense that without its Supra-Existence, nothing could exist.

Now acknowledging Amen-Renef, whose essence is unknown, we can enter the realms of the creation cycles, of which we are a part.

PART II : THE PRINCIPLES AND PRINCIPALS OF CREATION

Chapter 2 : The Animating Energies of The Universe

2.1 IN THE PRE-CREATION BEGINNING—NUN—NOTHINGNESS

Every Egyptian creation text begins with the same basic belief: that before the beginning of things, there was a liquidy primeval abyss—everywhere, endless, and without boundaries or directions. Egyptians called this cosmic ocean/watery chaos Nu/Ny/Nun—the un-polarized state of matter. Water is formless, and of itself it does not take on any shape; nor does it resist being shaped.

Scientists agree with the Ancient Egyptian description of the origin of the universe as being an abyss. Scientists refer to this abyss as 'neutron soup', where there are neither electrons nor protons; only neutrons forming one huge, extremely dense nucleus.

Such chaos, in the pre-creation state, was caused by the compression of matter; i.e. atoms did not exist in their normal states, but were squeezed so closely together that many atomic nuclei were crowded into a space previously occupied by a single normal atom. Under such conditions, the electrons of these atoms were squeezed out of their orbits and moved about freely, i.e. in a chaotic, degenerate state.

Nu/Ny/Nun is the "Subjective Being"; the symbol of the unformed, undefined, undifferentiated energy/matter, inert or inactive; the uncreated state before the creation – it cannot be the cause of its transformation.

The term "infinite", of course, is synonymous with "not finite", undefined, unlimited, unshaped, undifferentiated, and so on. This means that the energy/matter out of which all things are formed must be, in its essential state, unformed, undefined, undifferentiated, etc. If the material basis of the world had any essential definitions (formations), these would act as limiting factors to its ability to be transformed infinitely. Its essential lack of definition is an absolute requirement for God's creative omnipotence.

2.2 LET CREATION BEGIN

The condensed energy in the pre-creation neutron soup was continuously building up. This condensed energy reached the optimum concentration of buildup energy that led to its explosion and expansion outwardly, about 15 billion years ago.

The loud sound of this explosion is what caused the breakup of the constituent parts of the universe.

The Ancient Egyptian texts likewise repeatedly stressed that the divine commanding voice—meaning the Divine Sound was the cause of creation.

2.3 SOUND AND FORM

The earliest recovered Ancient Egyptian texts 5,000 years ago show the belief that the Word caused the creation of the World. The Egyptian *Book of the Coming Forth by Light* (wrongly and commonly translated as the *Book of the Dead*), the oldest written text in the world, states:

> *"I am the Eternal ... I am that which created the Word ... I am the Word ..."*

We also find, in the Book of the Divine Cow (found in the shrines of Tut-Ankh-Amen), that the heavens and their hosts came into existence merely by pronouncing words whose sound alone evokes things. As its name is pronounced, so the thing comes into being.

For the name is a reality; the thing itself. In other words: each particular sound has/is its corresponding form. Modern science has confirmed a direct relationship between sound wave frequency and form.

The word (any word) is, scientifically, a vibrational complex element which is a wave phenomenon characterized by movements of variable frequency and intensity. In other words, sound is caused by compressing air particles—by rearranging the spacing and movement of air particles, i.e. creating forms. Each sound wave frequency has its own geometrical corresponding form.

The divine sound transformed the potential inert energy/ matter in Nun into the parts of the universe as differentiated, orderly, structured kinetic energies in the form of objects, thoughts, forces, physical phenomena, etc.

Transforming one type of energy (potential) into another type (kinetic) made the universe come to life, in whole and in its constituent parts.

It is all a matter of energies.

2.4 ATAM—THE MANIFESTED COSMIC ENERGY

As we have seen, creation came out of the state of no-creation. The Egyptians called it Nun. None or nil also represents the pre-creation state of the universe. There is NO universe: NONE NILL ZERO. Such a state of the universe represents the Subjective Being—unformed, undefined, and undifferentiated energy/ matter. Its inert energy is inactive.

On the other hand, the creation state is orderly, formed, defined, and differentiated. The totality of the divine energy during the creation state is called Atam by the Egyptians.

Creation is the sorting out (giving definition to/bringing order to) all the chaos (the undifferentiated energy/matter and consciousness) of the primeval state. All of the Ancient Egyptian accounts of creation exhibited this with well-defined, clearly demarcated stages.

The first stage of creation was the self-creation of the Supreme Being as creator and Being, i.e. the passage from Subjective Being (Nu/Ny/Nun) to Objective Being (Atam). In simple human terms, this is equivalent to the moment that one passes from sleeping (unconscious state, subjective being) to being aware of oneself (gaining consciousness, objective being). It is like standing on solid ground.

This stage of creation was represented by the Egyptian sages as Atam/Atum rising out of Nu/Ny/Nun. In the Unas (so-called Pyramid) Texts, there is the following invocation:

> *Salutation to thee, Atam,*
> *Salutation to thee, he who comes into being by himself!*
> *Thou art high in this thy name High Mound,*
> *Thou comest into being in this thy name Khepri* (Becoming One). [§1587]

Atam means the *One-ness of all*; the complete. Atam is connected with the root, 'tam' or 'tamam', meaning *"to be complete"* or *"to make an end of"*.

In Ancient Egyptian texts Atam means this who completes or perfects, and in the Litany of Re, Atam is recognized as *the Complete One, the ALL*

The Ancient Egyptian texts emphasize that the Complete One contains all. The Ancient Egyptian text reads:

> *"I am many of names and many of forms, and my Being exists in every neter".*

Numerically, one is not a number, but the essence of the underlying principle of number; all other numbers being made of it. One represents Unity: the Absolute as unpolarized energy. Atam as the number One is neither odd nor even, but both. Atam is neither female nor male, but both.

Atam is the totality of the orderly energy matrix during the creation stage, while Nun is the disorderly energy compound—the Subjective Being. The total divine energy within the universe is called Nun in its chaotic state and Atam in its orderly creation and its point of state/process.

Atam represents the release, in an orderly sequence, of the existing energy within Nun, i.e. bringing it to life. This represents the Objective Being.

Nun and Atam are images of each other, like the numbers 0 and 1. 0 is nothing, nil; and 1 means "the all".

2.5 EXISTENCE OF THE ALL—THE BECOMING ONE

Creation is the sorting out (giving definition to/bringing order to) all the chaos (the undifferentiated energy/matter and consciousness) of the primeval state. All of the Ancient Egyptian accounts of creation exhibited this with well defined, clearly demarcated stages.

The seed of creation out of which everything originated is Atam. And, just as the plant is contained within the seed; so everything that is created in the universe is Atam, too.

Atam, the One who is the All, as the Master of the Universe, declares, in the Ancient Egyptian papyrus commonly known as the Bremner-Rhind Papyrus:

> *"When I manifested myself into existence, existence existed.*
> *I came into existence in the form of the Existent, which came*
> *into existence in the First Time.*

> *Coming into existence according to the mode of existence of the Existent, I therefore existed.*
> *And it was thus that the Existent came into existence".*

In other words, when the Master of the Universe came into existence, the whole of creation came into existence, because the Complete One contains the all.

2.6 NETERU—THE DIVINE ENERGIES

We just saw that when the Master of the Universe came into existence, the whole creation came into existence, because the Complete One contains the all.

The cycle of creation is caused and maintained by divine forces or energies. These energies like the perpetual cycle of creation go through a process of transformation from birth-life-aging-dying-death to rebirth. We, as human beings, have similar life forces that change throughout our lifetime. Our human bodies consist of numerous cycles that govern our life existence. All forces die out when we die.

The Egyptians called these divine forces neteru. The main theme of the universe is its cyclical nature. The NeTeRu are the forces of NaTuRe, which make the world go around—so to speak. To simply call them gods and goddesses gives a false impression.

The Divine energy that manifests itself in the creation cycle is defined by its constituent energy aspects, which were called neteru by the Ancient Egyptians. In order for creation to exist and to be maintained, this divine energy must be thought of in terms of male and female principles.

Therefore, Ancient Egyptians expressed the cosmic energy forces in the terms of netert (female principle) and neter (male principle).

The Egyptian word 'neter' (or nature or 'netjer') means *a power that is able to generate life and to maintain it when generated.* As all parts of creation go through the cycle of birth-life-death-rebirth, so do the driving energies, during the stages of this cycle. It is therefore that the Ancient Egyptian neteru, being divine energies, went (and continue to go) through the same cycle of birth-growth-death and renewal. Such understanding was common to all, as noted by Plutarch; that the multitude forces of nature (known as neteru) are born or created, subject to continuous changes, age and die, and are reborn.

We can give the example of the caterpillar that is born, lives, then builds its own cocoon, where it dies – or better yet, transforms into a butterfly which lays eggs, and on and on. What we have here is the cyclical transformation from one form/state of energy to another.

Another example is the water cycle—the water that evaporates, forming clouds that rain back to earth. It is all an orderly cyclical transformation of energies in various forms.

When you think of neteru not as *gods* and *goddesses* but as cosmic energy forces, one can see the Ancient Egyptian system as a brilliant representation of the universe. Philosophically, this cyclical, natural transformation is similar to our saying:

"The more things change, the more they stay the same".

In scientific circles, this is known as **the natural law of conservation of energy**, which is described as the principle that *energy is never consumed, but only changes form, and the total energy in a physical system, such as the universe, cannot be increased or diminished.*

2.7 MAAT: THE DIVINE ORDER

For the deeply religious people of Egypt, the creation of the universe was not a physical event that just happened. It was an orderly event that was pre-planned and executed according to an orderly Divine Law that governs the physical and metaphysical worlds. So, we read in the *Book of Knowing the Creations of Ra and Overcoming Apep* (Apophis), known as the *Bremner-Rhind Papyrus*:

> ***I had not yet found a place upon which I could stand. I conceived the Divine Plan of Law or Order (Maa) to make all forms. I was alone, I had not yet emitted Shu, nor had I yet emitted Tefnut, nor existed any other who could act together with me.***

Ma-at is the netert (goddess) that represents the principle of cosmic order, the concept by which not only men, but also the neteru (gods, goddesses) themselves, were governed and without which the neteru (gods, goddesses) are functionless.

2.8 THE UNIVERSAL ENERGY MATRIX AND EINSTEIN

This matrix of energies came as a result of the initial act of creation and the subsequent effects that created the universe. This matrix consists of an organized hierarchy. Each level of the hierarchy of existence is a theophany—a creation by the consciousness of the level of being above it. The self-contemplation by each stage of existence brings into being each lower stage. As such, the hierarchy of energies is interrelated, and each level is sustained by the level below it. This hierarchy of energies is set neatly into a vast matrix of deeply interfaced natural laws. It is both physical and metaphysical.

The Ancient and Baladi Egyptians made/make no distinction between a metaphysical state of being and one with a material body. Such a distinction is a mental illusion. We exist on a number of different levels at once, from the most physical to the most metaphysical. Einstein agreed with these same principles.

Since Einstein's relativity theory, it has been known and accepted that matter is a form of energy; a coagulation or condensation of energy. As a result, the natural law for the conservation of matter or mass similarly states that matter is neither created nor destroyed during any physical or chemical change.

Energy is made up of molecules rotating or vibrating at various rates of speed. In the "physical" world, molecules rotate at a very slow and constant rate of speed. That is why things appear to be solid, to our earthly senses: The slower the speed, the more dense or solid the thing. In the metaphysical (spirit) world, the molecules vibrate at a much faster rate or in an ethereal dimension where things are freer and less dense.

In this light, the universe is basically a hierarchy of energies at different orders of density. Our senses have some access to the densest form of energy, which is matter. The hierarchy of energies is interrelated, and each level is sustained by the level below it. This hierarchy of energies is set neatly into a vast matrix of deeply interfaced natural laws. It is both physical and metaphysical.

The universal energy matrix encompasses the world as the product of a complex system of relationships among people (living and dead), animals, plants, and natural and supernatural phenomena. This rationale is often called Animism because of its central premise that all things are animated (energized) by life forces. Each minute particle of everything is in constant motion – i.e. energized, as acknowledged in kinetic theory. In other words: everything is animated (energized)—animals, trees, rocks, birds – even the air, sun, and moon.

The faster form of energies—these invisible energies in the universe—are called spirits by many. Spirits/energies are organized at different orders of densities, which relates to the different speeds of molecules. These faster (invisible) energies inhabit certain areas, or are associated with particular natural phenomena.

Spirits (energies) exist in family-type groups (i.e., related to each other).

Energies may occupy, at will, a more condensed energy (matter) such as human, animal, plant, or any form. The spirit animates the human body at birth and leaves it at death. Sometimes more than one energy spirit enters a body.

We often hear that a person is 'not feeling himself/herself', or is 'temporarily insane', 'possessed', 'beside himself', or we hear of a person with multiple personalities. The energies (spirits) have an effect on all of us, to one degree or another.

The presence of energy in everything was long recognized by the Ancient and Baladi Egyptians. That there are cosmic energies (neteru) in every stone, mineral, wood, etc., is stated clearly in the Shabaka Stele (8th Century BCE):

> *"And so the neteru* (gods, goddesses)*entered into their bodies, in the form of every sort of wood, of every sort of mineral, as every sort of clay, as everything which grows upon him (meaning earth)".*

2.9 NETERU AND ANGELS

The neteru (gods, goddesses) are the divine energies/ powers/ forces that, through their actions and interactions, created and maintained (and continue to maintain) the universe.

The neteru (gods, goddesses) and their functions, were later acknowledged by others as *angels*. The Song of Moses in Deuteronomy (32:43), as found in a cave at Qumran near the Dead Sea, mentions the word *gods* in the *plural*:

> *"Rejoice, O heavens, with him; and do obeisance to him, ye gods".*

When the passage is quoted in the New Testament (Hebrews, 1:6), the word 'gods' is substituted with 'angels of God'.

The spheres of neteru (known also as angels and archangels, in Christianity) are hierarchical among the levels/realms of the universe .

2.10 NAME CALLING

As stated earlier, Egyptian creation texts repeatedly stress the belief of creation by the Word. We find that in the Book of the Divine Cow (found in the shrines of TutAnkh- Amen), Re creates the heavens and its hosts merely by pronouncing some words whose sound alone evokes the names of things—and these things then appear at his bidding. As its name is pronounced, so the thing comes into being. For the name is a reality; the thing itself.

The role of the name in Ancient and Baladi Egypt was not, as per our modern-day thinking, a *mere label*. The name of a neter, person, animal, or principle represents a resume or synopsis of the qualities of that person or object. To know and pronounce the real name of a neter (god, goddess), man, or animal is to exercise power over it. It is therefore that Ancient and Baladi Egyptians have real "secret" names for everybody and everything, in order to protect the person and the thing.

The traditional story of the *Mystery of the Divine Name* is found on an Ancient Egyptian papyrus now in the Turin Museum. In the story, Re refused to tell even the most beloved Being, Isis, his real (secret) name. The events of the story end with Re "divulging" his "secret" name as *Amen*. It should be noted that Amen means *secret/hidden*. In other words: under all difficult circumstances, Re (as a model for all) did not divulge his real name, but only stated that his secret name was [Amen] *secret*.

The learned and most trusted people in an Egyptian community knew/know the great real (or secret) names of the neteru (gods, goddesses) and other cosmic forces, and used this knowledge to maintain order in the world.

The real names of the deities (gods, goddesses) were kept secret. The real name was/is imbued with magical powers and properties. To know and pronounce the real name of a neter/netert (god/goddess) is to exercise power over it. To guard the cosmic power of the deity, the Ancient Egyptians often used "names" with religious connotations. 'Baal' simply means Lord or Ruler, and so we hear of the Baal or the Baalat (Lady) of such-and-such a city. Similarly, a deity will be called Melek, meaning King. So, too, Adon; which means Lord or Master. Melqart meant King of the City. Other "names" meanings favored by the gods or granted by the gods were translated to Latin as Fortunatus, Felix, Donatus, Concessus, and so on.

2.11 THE CREATION CYCLE

The system of creation is a system of necessary emanation, procession, or irradiation accompanied by necessary aspiration or reversion-to-source. All the forms and phases of Existence flow from the Divinity, and all strive to return thither and to remain there.

As a consequence of the Big Bang, the expulsion forces, which cause all galaxies to move outwardly, are being opposed by the gravitational/contractional forces which pull the galaxies together. At the present time, the outwardly forces exceed the contractional forces; and therefore, the limits of the universe are still expanding.

Scientists tell us that at a certain point in time in the future, the universe will stop expanding and will start getting smaller. The microwave radiation from the Big Bang fireball (which is still rushing around) will start squashing down, and will heat up and change color again until it becomes visible once more. The sky will become red, and will then turn orange, yellow, white … and will end in the Big Crunch; i.e., all the matter and all the radiation in the universe will come crashing together into one unit.

The Big Crunch is not the end in itself; for the reunited, crunched universe (neutron soup) will have the potential for a new creation, which is called the Big Bounce.

So it is not surprising that the Ancient Egyptian texts have also described, in their usual Egyptian symbolic terms, The Big Crunch and the Big Bounce.

The Egyptian coffin texts, Spell 130, tells us that:

> *"After the millions of years of differentiated creation the chaos before creation will return. Only the Complete One [Atam] and Aus-Ra will remain. . . no longer separated in space and time".*

The Ancient Egyptian text tells us two points. The first is the return of the created universe to chaos at the end of the creation cycle, which signifies the Big Crunch. The second point is the potential for a new cyclical rebirth of the universe as symbolized by the presence of Aus-Ra.

Let us pause here for a few minutes to learn about what has been advertised as "names" of deities in Egypt.

Aus-Ra consists of two words. The word **Aus** means *the power of,* or *the root of.* As such, Aus-Ra means *the power of Ra;* meaning: the *re-birth of Ra.*

The principle that makes life come from apparent death was/is called Aus-Ra, who symbolizes the power of renewal. The main theme of the Ancient Egyptian texts is the cyclical nature of creation being born, living, dying, and regenerating again.

2.12 SIRIUS AND COMPANION: CENTER OF CREATION

During the very remote periods of the Ancient Egyptian history,

Isis was associated with the star Sirius, the brightest star in heaven, which was called (like her) *the Great Provider*. Egypt's ingenious and very accurate calendar was based on the observation and study of Sirius movements in the sky.

Numerous monuments can be found throughout Ancient Egyptian sites, attesting to their full awareness and knowledge of cosmology and astronomy. A systematic kind of astronomical observation began in Ancient Egypt at a very early time. The Ancient Egyptians compiled information, making charts of the constellations based on observations and recordings of the *star that follows Sirius.*

The Greeks, Romans, and other ancient sources confirmed that the Egyptians regarded Sirius as the great central fire about which our solar system orbits. Sirius' movements are intimately associated with another companion star. Sirius and its companion are revolving around their common center of gravity or, in other words, are revolving around each other. Sirius' diameter is less than twice the diameter of our sun. Its companion, however, has a diameter only about three times the diameter of Earth, yet it weighs about 250,000 times as much as the Earth. Its material is packed together so tightly that it is about 5,000 times as dense as lead. Such a compression of matter means that Sirius' companion's atoms do not exist in their normal states, but are squeezed so closely together that many atomic nuclei are crowded into a space previously occupied by a single normal atom; i.e., the electrons of these atoms are squeezed out of their orbits and move about freely (a degenerate state). This is the Egyptian Nun; the neutron soup—the origin of all matter and energy in the universe.

The movement of Sirius' companion on its own axis, and around Sirius, upholds all creation in space; and as such is considered the starting point of creation. Ancient Egyptian records state that the commencement of the Sothic period corresponded with the beginning of the world—the beginning of a zodiac cycle of about 26,000 years.

Chapter 3 : The Pictorial Metaphysical Images

3.1 PICTORIAL SYMBOLISM OF THE NETERU

In order to represent and convey the scientific and philosophical meanings of the neteru (gods, goddesses), the Egyptian devised and utilized a thoughtful system of visual ideographs.

Scientists concur on the scientific/metaphysical realities of pictorial images, since they concur with how human beings process information received from the five senses to the brain through visualized images.

A symbol, by definition, is not what it represents, but what it stands for – what it suggests. A symbol reveals to the mind a reality other than itself. Words convey information; symbols evoke understanding.

A chosen symbol represents that function or principle on all levels, simultaneously—from the simplest, most obvious physical manifestation of that function to the most abstract and metaphysical. Without recognizing the simple fact of the intent of symbolism, we will continue to be ignorant of the wealth of Egyptian knowledge and wisdom.

In Egyptian symbolism, the precise role of the neteru (gods, goddesses) was revealed in many ways: by dress, headdress, crowns, feathers, animals, plants, color, position, size, gesture, sacred object, or type of symbolic equipment (e.g., flail, scepter, staff, ankh, etc.).

3.2 HOW DO EGYPTIAN DEPICTIONS REFLECT METAPHYSICAL CONCEPTS?

3.2.i – Man's depiction signifies The Universe—Earthly and Divine

So many phrases are being used throughout the world, which consistently state that the human being is made in the image of God – i.e. a miniature universe – and that to understand the universe is to understand oneself; and vice versa.

Yet, no culture has ever practiced the above principle like the Ancient Egyptians. Central to their complete understanding of the universe was the knowledge that man was made in the image of God and, as such, man represented the image of all creation.

Consistent with such thinking, a depicted human being represents both the universe as a whole as well as the human being on Earth. The difference between the two will be clear in each particular context.

3.2.ii – Animal Symbolism

Egyptians' careful observations and profound knowledge of the natural world enabled them to identify certain animals with specific qualities that could symbolize certain divine functions and principles in a particularly pure and striking fashion. As such, certain animals were chosen as symbols for these particular aspects of divinity.

When you say someone is loyal, the word 'loyal' is so vague. But if you say 'loyal as a dog', you leave no doubt about your intent. This is the power of animal analogy.

The animal or animal-headed neteru (gods, goddesses) were symbolic expressions of a deep spiritual understanding. When a total animal is presented in Ancient Egypt, it represents a particular function/attribute in its purest form. When an animal-headed figure is presented, it conveys that particular function/

attribute in the human being. The two forms of Anubis, in the two illustrations shown here, clearly distinguishes these two aspects.

This third form is the opposite of animal-headed human. In this case, we have a human-headed bird—that is the Ba—representing the body/soul hovering over the body.

The depiction of the Ba, then, is the divine aspect of the terrestrial. The Ba is depicted as a stork. The stork is known for its migrating and homing instinct, and is also known worldwide as the bird that carries newborn babies to their new families. The stork returns to its own nest with consistent precision—hence, it is a migratory bird is the perfect choice to represent the soul.

[More examples of animal symbolism are found in *Egyptian Divinities*, by this same author.]

3.2.iii – Accessories, Emblems, color ,etc.

In Egyptian symbolism, the precise role of the neteru (gods/goddesses) are revealed in many ways: by dress, headdress, crown, feather, animal, plant, color, position, size, gesture, sacred object (e.g., flail, scepter, staff, ankh), etc. This symbolic language represents a wealth of physical, physiological, psychological and spiritual data in the presented symbols.

3.2.iv – Action forms

Practically all figures on the walls of Egyptian monuments are in profile form, indicative of action and interaction between the various symbolic figures. A wide variety of actions in the forms are evident.

[More detailed information about the subjects of this chapter are to be found in several publications by Moustafa Gadalla.]

Chapter 4 : Egyptian Creation Process Accounts

4.1 VARIOUS ASPECTS/FORMS OF MANIFESTATION

As was shown earlier the universal matrix of energies came as a result of the initial act of creation and the subsequent effects that created the universe. This matrix consists of an organized hierarchy. Each level of the hierarchy of existence is a theophany—a creation by the consciousness of the level of being above it. As such, the hierarchy of energies is interrelated, and each level is sustained by the level below it. This hierarchy of energies is set neatly into a vast matrix of deeply interfaced natural laws. It is both physical and metaphysical.

The origin of the world and the nature of the neteru (gods, goddesses) who took part in its creation were subjects of constant interest to the Egyptians.

Ancient Egyptians had four main cosmological teaching centers at Heliopolis, Memphis, Thebes, and Khmunu (Hermopolis). Each center revealed one of the principle phases or aspects of genesis. As such creation accounts are all consistent with the orderly formation of/within the universal energy matrix.

4.2 EGYPTIAN COSMOLOGY AND ALLEGORIES

The totality of the Egyptian civilization was built upon a complete and precise understanding of universal laws. This profound understanding manifested itself in a consistent, coherent, and interrelated system where art, science, philosophy and religion were intertwined, and were employed simultaneously in a single organic Unity.

Egyptian cosmology is based on coherent scientific and philosophical principles. The cosmological knowledge of Ancient Egypt was expressed in a story form, which is a superior means for expressing both physical and metaphysical concepts. Any good writer or lecturer knows that stories are better than exposition for explaining the behavior of things, because the relationships of parts to each other (and to the whole) are better maintained by the mind. Information alone is useless unless it is transformed into understanding.

The Egyptian sagas transformed common factual nouns and adjectives (indicators of qualities) into proper but conceptual nouns. These were, in addition, personified so that they could be woven into coherent and meaningful narratives. Personification is based on their knowledge that man was made in the image of God and, as such, man represented the created image of all creation.

Allegories are an intentionally chosen means for communicating knowledge. Allegories dramatize cosmic laws, principles, processes, relationships and functions, and express them in an easy to understand way. Once the inner meanings of the allegories have been revealed, they become marvels of simultaneous scientific and philosophical completeness and conciseness. The more they are studied, the richer they become. The 'inner dimension' of the teachings embedded into each story are capable of revealing several layers of knowledge, according to the stage of development of the listener. The "secrets" are revealed as one evolves higher. The higher we get, the more we see. It is always there.

The Egyptians (Ancient and present-day Baladi) did/do not

believe their allegories as historical facts. They believed IN them, in the sense that they believed in the truth beneath the stories.

Throughout this book, several subjects will be explained in story forms using four personified concepts: Isis, Osiris, Horus, and Seth. Four of such subjects will be:

> 1 – The solar and lunar principles as represented by Isis and Osiris.

> 2 – The four elements of the world (water, fire, earth, and air) equated to Osiris, Seth, Isis and Horus, respectively.

> 3 – The model societal framework is expressed in the legendary tale of Osiris and Isis, their son Horus, and his uncle, Seth.

> 4 – Numerology and trigonometry, as well as the trinity/triad/triangle cosmic role, as described into the relationship between the father [Osiris], mother [Isis], and son [Horus] are analogous to the right-angle triangle 3:4:5.

The Egyptian well-crafted mystery plays are an intentionally chosen means for communicating knowledge.

Meaning and the mystical experience are not tied to a literal interpretation of events. Once the inner meanings of the narratives have been revealed, they become marvels of simultaneous scientific and philosophical completeness and conciseness. The more they are studied, the richer they become.

And, rooted in the narrative as it is, the part can never be mistaken for the whole; nor can its functional significance be forgotten or distorted.

4.3 THE THREE PRIMARY PHASES OF THE CREATION CYCLE

The sequence of the creation cycle is delineated into three primary phases, in the Ancient Egyptian texts. The very same delineations were later on duplicated in Sufi (and other) writings.

The followings are three main Ancient Egyptian sources for such triple delineations:

A- Pyramid Texts: Consistent with the theme of three phases of the creation cycle, we find that, as far back as at least 5,000 years ago, the "Pyramid" Texts reveals the existence of three companies of neteru (gods,goddesses), and each company consisted of 9 neteru (gods, goddesses). Throughout the "Pyramid" Texts, frequent mention is made of one group, or of 2 or 3 groups, of 9 neteru (gods, goddesses).

The Egyptian texts speak of three Enneads, each representing a phase in the creation cycle. Nine is the number of each phase—each phase begets the following phase in 9 terms.

The first (Great) Ennead represents the conceptual or divine stage. This is governed by Re.

The second Ennead represents the manifestation stage. This is governed by Osiris.

The third Ennead represents the return to the Source, combining both Re and Osiris.

In The Book of the Coming Forth By Light, both the souls of Osiris and Re meet and are united to form an entity, described so eloquently:

I am His Two Souls in his Twins.

B- Litany of Re: After a brief preface, the Litany opens with seventy-five invocations to the Forms of Re, followed by a series of prayers and hymns in which the identity of Re and Osiris is constantly stressed.

The perpetual cycle of Osiris and Re dominates the Ancient Egyptian texts. The first leg is the manifestation of Re in his various forms. The second leg is the manifestation of Osiris in his forms. The third and final leg occurs in the Netherlands to join together and resurrect as a new ReHerakhuti of the Two Horizons.

C- Leiden Papyrus J350: This surviving Ancient Egyptian document is dated to at least since the Old Kingdom (2575–2150 BCE), a copy of which was reproduced during the reign of Ramses II in the 13th century BCE .

The Leiden Papyrus J350 consists of an extended composition describing the principle aspects of the ancient creation narratives. The system of numeration in the Papyrus identifies the principle/aspect of creation and matches each one with its symbolic number.

The manuscript is divided into a series of numbered "stanzas". Each is entitled "Mansions [of the moon], number xx".

The numbering system of this Egyptian Papyrus, by itself, is significant. They are numbered in three tiers—1 to 9 – and then the powers 10, 20, 30, to 90, to constitute the energetic foundations of physical forms—and the third tier is numbered in the 100s.

This numbering system shows the three phases of the creation cycle:

1. The Conceiving Phase/Ennead whose theme is the objectification of a circumscribed area of undifferentiated energy/matter, wherein the world will be manifested.

2. The Orderly Manifestation Phase/Ennead deals with the creation of the noumenal and phenomenal planes—the two grand subdivisions of the manifested world.

3. The Reunification Phase/Ennead whose theme is the return to the Source and subsequent reunification process that leads to a NEW Alpha.

[For the details of the three phases of creation cycle see *Egyptian Alphabetical Letters of Creation Cycle* by Moustafa Gadalla.]

Chapter 5 : Numerology of the Creation Process

5.1 ALL IS NUMBER—NUMBER MYSTICISM

The Ancient Egyptians had a scientific and organic system of observing reality. Modern-day science is based on observing everything dead (inanimate). Modern physical formulas in our science studies almost always exclude the vital phenomena throughout statistical analyses. For the Ancient and Baladi Egyptians, the universe—in whole and in part—is animated.

In the animated world of Ancient Egypt, numbers did not simply designate quantities; but instead were considered to be concrete definitions of energetic formative principles of nature. The Egyptians called these energetic principles neteru (gods, goddesses).

For Egyptians, numbers were not just odd and even—they were male and female. Every part of the universe was/is a male or a female. There is no *neutral* (a thing). Unlike in English, where something is always *he, she,* or *it*; in Egypt there was only *he* or *she*.

Egyptians manifested their knowledge of number mysticism in all aspects of their lives. The evidence that Egypt possessed this knowledge is concrete. Some examples:

1 – The concept of animated numbers in Ancient Egypt were eloquently referred to by Plutarch, in *Moralia Vol. V*, describing the 3:4:5 triangle:

The upright, therefore, may be likened to the male, the base to the female, and the hypotenuse to the child of both, and so Osiris may be regarded as the origin, Isis as the recipient, and Horus as perfected result. Three is the first perfect odd number: four is a square whose side is the even number two; but five is in some ways like to its father, and in some ways like to its mother, being made up of three and two. And panta [all] is a derivative of pente [five], and they speak of counting as "numbering by fives".

Five makes a square of itself.

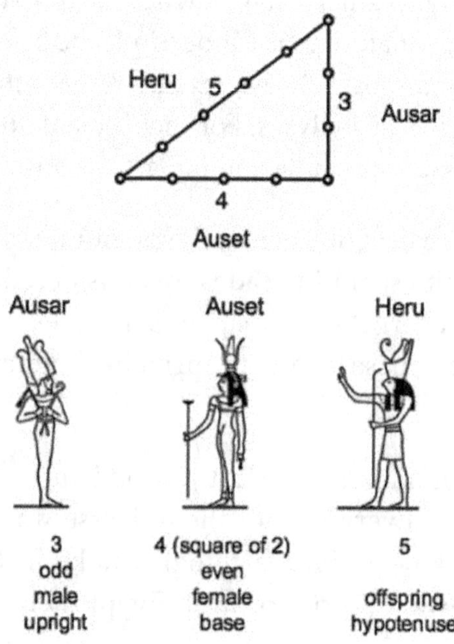

The vitality and the interactions between these numbers show how they are male and female, active and passive, vertical and horizontal, etc.

2 – Plutarch noted that One, for the Egyptians, was not an (odd) number when he wrote: *three is the first perfect odd number*. For the Egyptians, one was not a number, but the essence of the

underlying principle of number; all other numbers being made of it. One represents Unity: the Absolute as unpolarized energy. One is neither odd nor even, but both; because, if added to an odd number, it makes it even, and vice-versa. So it combines the opposites of odd and even, and all the other opposites in the universe. Unity is a perfect, eternal, undifferentiated consciousness.

3 – The heading of the Ancient Egyptian papyrus known as the *Rhind* (the so-called "Mathematical") *Papyrus* (1848-1801 BCE) reads:

> **Rules for inquiring into nature and for knowing all that exists, every mystery, every secret.**

The intent is very clear—that Ancient Egyptians believed in and set the rules for numbers and their interactions (so called mathematics) as the basis for **"all that exists".**

4 – The Ancient Egyptian mode of calculation had a direct relationship with natural processes, as well as metaphysical ones. Even the language employed in the Egyptian papyri serves to promote this sense of vitality; of living interactions. We see this understanding as an example in Item No. 38 of the Egyptian papyrus known as the *Rhind* (so-called "Mathematical") *Papyrus*, which reads:

> **I go three times into the hekat** (a bushel, unit of volume), **a seventh of me is added to me and I return fully satisfied.**

5 – The famous Ancient Egyptian hymn of Leiden Papyrus J350 confirms that number symbolism had been practiced in Egypt at least since the Old Kingdom (2575-2150 BCE). The Leiden Papyrus consists of an extended composition describing the principle aspects of the ancient creation narratives. The system of enumeration, in the Papyrus, identifies the principle/aspect of creation and matches each one with its symbolic number.

This Egyptian Papyrus consists of 27 stanzas numbered from 1 to 9; then from 10 to 90 in tens; then from 100 to 900 in hundreds. Only 21 have been preserved. The first word of each is a sort of pun on the number under concern.

Some parts of the Leiden Papyrus will be discussed in conjunction with number mysticism/evaluation in the next chapters. However, a complete analysis is found in *Egyptian Alphabetical Letters of Creation Cycle* by Moustafa Gadalla.

6 – The Ancient Egyptian name for the largest temple in Egypt, namely the Karnak Temple complex, is **Apet-sut**, which means **Enumerator of the Places**. The temple's name speaks for itself. This temple started in the Middle Kingdom in Ca. 1971 BCE, and was added to continuously for the next 1,500 years. The design and enumeration, in this temple, are consistent with the creation numerical codes.

The Egyptian concept of number symbolism was subsequently popularized in the West by and through the Egyptian-educated Pythagoras (ca. 580–500 BCE). It is a known fact that Pythagoras studied for about 20 years in Egypt.

Pythagoras and his immediate followers left nothing of their own writing. Yet, Western Academia attributed to Pythagoras the so-called *Pythagoreans*, an open-ended list of major achievements. They were issued a blank check by Western academia.

Pythagoras and his followers are said to see numbers as divine concepts – ideas of the God that created a universe of infinite variety, and satisfying order, to a numerical pattern.

The same principles were stated more than 13 centuries before Pythagoras' birth in the heading of the Egyptian's *Rhind Papyrus*, which promises:

Rules for inquiring into nature and for knowing all that exists, every mystery, every secret.

Some of the numbers and their symbolic significance will be described briefly in the following chapters.

5.2 NATURAL PROGRESSION—THE ORDERLY SEQUENCE OF THE CREATION CYCLE

Creation is the sorting out (giving definition to/bringing order to) all the chaos (the undifferentiated energy/matter and consciousness) of the primeval state. **All of the Ancient Egyptian accounts of creation exhibited this with orderly, well defined, clearly demarcated stages.** The first stage of creation was represented by the Egyptians as Atam/Atum/Atem, emerging out of Nu/Ny/ Nun—the neutron soup.

Throughout the Ancient Egyptian texts, we consistently find how one state of being develops (or better yet, emerges) into the next state of being. And we always find that any two consecutive states are images of each other. Not only is that scientifically correct; but it is orderly, natural, and poetic. The Egyptians were famous for writing these scientific and philosophical subjects in poetic forms.

Numbers conform to the arrangement of natural things; for most natural things were established by the Creator in orders. Numbers are neither abstractions nor entities in themselves. **Numbers are names applied to the functions and principles upon which the universe is created and maintained.**

5.3 THE UNIVERSAL NUMBER TWO—ISIS, THE FEMALE PRINCIPLE

We have seen how an orderly creation in the form of Atam, the Complete One, emerged out of the pre-creation chaotic state of the Nun—the nothingness.

We have also seen how one state of being develops or emerges into the next state of being, and how every two consecutive stages are images of each other. Nun and Atam are images of each other, like the numbers 0 and 1—0 is nothing, nil, and 1 means the all.

The first thing that developed from the light of unity of the Complete One was the force of Active Reason, as He made two arise from one, by repetition.

This divine active reason thought is the first 'thing' of which existence may proceed as the act, offspring, and image of the first—Atam. The ability to conceive—both mentally and physically—was naturally represented by the female principle Isis, being the feminine side of Atam's unity. This was confirmed plainly in Plutarch's writings, where he wrote in his *Moralia Vol. V*:

> *". . ., since, because of the force of Reason. Isis turns herself to this thing or that and is receptive of all manner of shapes and forms."*

It is Isis being this Divine-Mind (or Divine-Intellection, or Divine-Intellectual-Principle) that begins the existence of Plurality, Complexity, or Multiplicity.

The relationship between the master of the universe—The Complete One—and the mother of creation is best described in musical terms. The relationship between Atam—the Complete One—and his female image (Isis) is like the relationship between the sound of a note and its octave note. Consider a string of a given length as unity. Set it vibrating; it produces a sound. Stop the string at its midpoint and set it vibrating. The frequency of vibrations produced is double that given by the whole string, and the tone is raised by one octave. The string length has been divided by two; and the number of vibrations per second has been multiplied by two: one half (1:2) as created its mirror opposite (2:1), 2/1. This harmonic relationship is represented by Atam and Isis.

Isis' number is two, which symbolizes the power of multiplicity, the female mutable, receptacle, horizontal, representing the basis of everything.

In Ancient Egyptian thinking, Isis as the number two is the image of the first principle—the divine intellect.

The relation of the intellect to the Complete One, Atam, is like the relation of the light of the sun effusing from the sun. The Ancient Egyptian texts describe Isis as being the divine sunshine, for she is called:

- *The daughter of the universal Lord.*
- *The female Re.*
- *The Light-giver in heaven with Re.*

Isis, then, is the emanated energy from the Complete One. As the female principle in the universe, only she can conceive and deliver the created universe.

In other words, Isis is the image of the cosmic creative impulse as recognized by the term Re. Thus, when speaking of Re, the Ancient Egyptian text says:

"Thou art the bodies of Isis."

This implies that Re, the creative energy, appears also in the different aspects of the cosmic female principle Isis. As such, Isis is recognized as:

-*The female Re.*
-*The Lady of the beginning of time.*
-*The prototype of all beings.*

Isis is recognized in the Ancient Egyptian texts as the God-Mother.

How loving Isis is—our God-Mother. She—the female principle—is the matrix of the created universe – 'matrix' being a motherly term, mater-x.

On the intellectual level, the first thought is to devise an orderly plan. The Ancient Egyptians emphasized the orderly and harmonic nature of the creation process, with Maat representing the Divine Order and Harmony. Maat is one of the manifestations of the female principle Isis.

So the Ancient Egyptian papyrus, known as the Bremner-

Rhind Papyrus, explains to us what the plan is:

> *"I conceived in my own heart; there came into being a vast number of forms of divine beings as the forms of children and the forms of their children."*

The first step to start creation was to conceive the concept of the multiple (divine beings) out of the One. The God-Mother Isis conceived the plan—metaphysically or intellectually—in her loving heart. This is both eloquent and poetic, because the heart was/is considered to be a symbol of intellectual perceptions, consciousness, and moral courage. Isis, as such, is also recognized as the **Mighty Heart.**

How eloquent that the Divine Mother Isis, being the womb of the universe, is also the one who conceived the creation plan and then delivers its parts; being *her children and their children.*

The Ancient Egyptian texts emphasize an orderly sequence of creation which is basically a system of necessary emanation, procession, or irradiation accompanied by necessary aspiration or reversion-to-source. All the forms and phases of Existence flow from the Divinity, and all strive to return thither and to remain there.

5.4 THE UNIVERSAL NUMBER THREE—OSIRIS, THE MALE PRINCIPLE

Now, with the plan of creation being conceived in the Divine Reason, the next logical step is to bring it to life. Therefore, Isis—the Divine-Thinking – engenders a power appropriate to the realization of its Thought. The bringing to life or animation of the creation plan is brought on by the All Soul, or Universal Soul of the All. The universal soul was represented in Ancient Egypt by Osiris, the third in the sequence of creation, and the number 3 was communicated through him. Osiris is the eternal emanation and image of the Second Hypostasis, the Intellectual-Principle.

Every stage of creation tends to engender an image of itself. It tends also to rejoin the next highest, of which it is itself a shadow or lower manifestation—for Isis is an image of the first principle, and her shadow is Osiris. How enlightening!

In the orderly sequence of creation, it was the female principle Isis who, after conceiving the plan, gave life to it. As such, Isis is called:

- *Isis, the Bestower of Life.*
- *Isis, the Lady of Life.*
- *Isis, the Giver of Life.*
- *Isis, the dweller in Neteru.*

5.5 THE UNIVERSAL TRINITY & DUALITY

As we have seen, it takes three components to create and bring something to life. So the prototype of generations encompasses three elements of the Creator Trinity, which are represented in the briefest description.

The first is The One, or First Existent—called Atam by the Egyptians; The Complete One—the One who is the all.

The second is the feminine principle called Isis which contains the Divine Mind, or First Thinker and Thought – the place of metaphysical and physical conception—the womb, the chamber, the entire universe.

The third is the masculine, animated, lively, dynamic, energetic principle called Osiris, known as the Universal Soul.

The Ancient Egyptians recognized the significance of trinity in the creation process. As such, Ancient Egyptian texts rendered the trinity as a unity expressed by the singular pronoun: it is the Three that are Two that are One.

The Triad is The Divinity, and is Divine. It is the expression of the outgoing energy of the Divinity. Such is eloquently expressed in the Ancient Egyptian text, known as the *Bremner-Rhind Papyrus*:

> *I was anterior to the Two Anteriors that I made,*
> *for I had priority over the Two Anteriors that I made,*
> *for my name was anterior to theirs,*
> *for I made them anterior to the Two Anteriors...*

The Egyptian text shows us that Unity, becoming conscious of itself, creates polarized energy – two new elements, each of which share in the nature of the One and of the Other. In other words, each of the female and male principles partakes of the other.

On the intellectual level, the female principle is both passive and active, for Isis conceives the plan in a passive mode, then provides life to the plan; thus reflecting her activeness as an extension of her passiveness; i.e. the intellect and world soul stand in the relation to active and passive intellect.

Intellect is as it is: always the same, resting in a static activity. This is a feminine attribute. Movement towards it and around it is the work of Soul, proceeding from Intellect to Soul and making Soul intellectual; not making another nature between Intellect and Soul.

And on the soul level, Isis is the passive and Osiris the active soul.

Again and again, we find the sequence of creation is based on one stage being the natural progression as well as the image of the following stage—and in reverse. From active-passive to passive-active is the chain reaction (so to speak) of creation.

Time is presented as the 'life' of the Soul in contrast to Eternity, which is the mode of existence of Intellect. However, Soul is an entity that spans various levels of reality, and we find that, on occasion, the highest aspect, at least, of Soul is largely assimilated to intellect.

The relation of the soul to the intellect is like the relation of the light of the moon to the light of the sun. Just as when the moon becomes full from the light of the sun, its light becomes an imitation of the light of the sun in the same way when the soul receives the effusion from the intellect, when its virtues become perfect and its acts imitate the acts of the intellect. When its virtues become perfect, then it knows its essence or self and the reality of its substance.

The combined forces of the divine mind and divine soul make the creation of the natural world possible. Isis as the Divine-Intellectual-Principle has two Acts: that of upward contemplation of The One and that of 'generation' towards the lower All-Soul. Likewise, the All-Soul has two Acts: it at once contemplates the Intellectual Principle and 'generates' (in the bounty of its own perfection) the Nature-Looking and Generative Soul, whose operation it is to generate or fashion the lower, material Universe upon the model of the Divine-Thoughts; the 'Ideas' laid up within the Divine-Mind. The All-Soul is the mobile cause of movement as well as of Form (or material or sense-grasped Universe) which is the Soul's Act and emanation, image, and 'shadow'.

With the combined forces of female and male energies, the creation plan can come to life.

5.6 THE UNIVERSAL NUMBER FIVE—HORUS, THE PHENOMENON

Two symbolizes the power of multiplicity—the female, mutable receptacle – while Three symbolizes the male. This was the music of the spheres—the universal harmonies played out between these two primal male and female universal symbols of Osiris and Isis, whose heavenly marriage produced the child Horus (number 5).

All phenomena without exception are polar in nature, and treble in principle. Therefore, five is the key to understanding the manifested universe which Plutarch explained in the Egyptian context,

> *...And panta (all) is a derivative of pente (five)...*

The significance and function of number five, in Ancient Egypt, is indicated by the manner in which it was written. The number five in Ancient Egypt was written as two ?? above three ? ? ?, (or, sometimes, as a five-pointed star). In other words, number five (the son–Horus) is the result of the relationship between number two (the mother–Isis) and number three (the father–Osiris).

5.7 THE NUMERICAL SEQUENCE OF CREATION 2,3,5 ...
THE SUMMATION SERIES

The sequence of numerical creation of Isis followed by Osiris followed by Horus is 2,3,5, etc.

It is a progressive series, where you start with the two primary numbers in the Ancient Egyptian system, i.e. 2 and 3. Then you add their total to the preceding number, and on and on. Any figure is the sum of the two preceding ones. The series would therefore be:

2
3
5 (3+2)
8 (5+3)
13 (8+5)
21 (13+8)
34 (21+13)
55 (34+21)
89, 144, 233, 377, 610, . . .

The Summation Series is reflected throughout nature. The number of seeds in a sunflower, the petals of any flower, the arrangement of pine cones, the growth of a nautilus shell, – all follow the same pattern of these series.

[See more information about this Summation series and its use in Ancient Egypt for at least 4,500 years in *The Ancient Egyptian Metaphysical Architecture* by Moustafa Gadalla.]

Chapter 6 : The Dualistic Nature

6.1 THE DUALISTIC NATURE OF CREATION—THE TWO OF THE ONE

The world, as we know it, is held together by a law that is based on the balanced dual nature of all things (wholes, units). Among noticeable polarized pairs are: male and female, odd and even, negative and positive, active and passive, light and darkness, yes and no, true and false—each pair represents a different aspect of the same fundamental principle of polarity. And each aspect partakes of the nature of unity and of the nature of duality.

The most eloquent expression of the dual nature is present in the Ancient Egyptian text, known as the *Bremner-Rhind Papyrus*:

> *"I was anterior to the Two Anteriors that I made, for I had priority over the Two Anteriors that I made, for my name was anterior to theirs, for I made them anterior to the Two Anteriors ..."*

6.2 ARCHETYPAL ANIMAL—TWO-HEADED SERPENT NEHEB KAU

The serpent represents the dualizing principle; the ability of One to divide into Two.

Looking at a serpent, it represents Unity, with its undifferentiated length.

It is the Unity that contains the power that results in duality.

The serpent, which is a remarkable individualistic animal, bears both a forked tongue (verbal duality) and a double penis (sexual duality).

The serpent, being the most flexible animal, represents the provider of all the various forms of creation.

Neheb Kau—meaning *the provider of forms/attributes/qualities*—was the name given to the serpent representing the primordial serpent/spiral in Ancient Egypt.

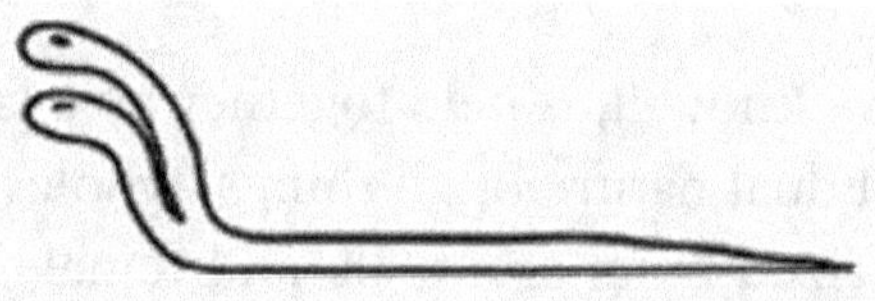

Neheb Kau is depicted as a two-headed serpent, indicative of the dual spiral nature of the universe.

6.3 MAIN APPLICATIONS OF THE DUALITY PRINCIPLE

The universal dual nature of creation manifests itself in various applications, as identified in Ancient Egypt.

Each dualizing aspect of the creation process is represented by two divine attributes—neteru. Depending on each specific aspect, the dualizing neteru [but always a solar and lunar combination] may be:

- A female and a male
- 2 females
- 2 males
- 2 halves of unisex

A very brief overview of sample Egyptian applications are shown here for three areas:

A- Creation—Formative Aspects

B- Unification Aspects

C- Cyclical Aspects

6.3.A DUALITIES WITH CREATION /FORMATIVE ASPECTS

6.3.A.i *Pre creation Twin gendered Dualities*

Egyptian texts state that Nun—the pre-creation chaos— possessed characteristics that were identified with four pairs of primordial powers/forces. Each pair represents the primeval dual-gendered twins—the masculine/feminine aspects.

The four males of the pairs are represented as frogs. The four females of the pairs are represented as serpents. The eight beings are depicted with their legs tied, indicative of their essential nature as being action; but while in the subjective realm (before creation), they are inert. Having the legs tied represents their potential energies. [more about the significance of animal symbolism are in other publications by same author, such as Egyptian Divinities.]

6.3.A.ii *Shu and Tefnut*

The dual Shu and Tefnut represent the initial act of creation forming the universal bubble The pair of Shu and Tefnut represented as a husband and wife is the characteristically Egyptian way of expressing duality and polarity. This dual nature was manifested in Ancient Egyptian texts and traditions, according to recovered archaeological findings.

The most ancient texts of the Old Kingdom, namely the Pyramid Texts §1652, express the dual nature:

...and though didst spit out as Shu, and didst spit out as Tefnut.

This is a very powerful analogy because we use the term "spitting image" to mean *exactly like the origin*.

The Ancient Egyptian concept of the universe is like a box. The first thing the Divine created is a kind of bubble in what is otherwise an infinite ocean of water. The sky is the skin of the infinite ocean that contains what we call the atmosphere, which was caused by two forces that the Ancient Egyptians called Shu and Tefnut. Both Shu (heat) and Tefnut (water/moisture) mean 'atmosphere'. Nun (the pre-creation cosmic ocean) is the root out of which Shu and Tefnut were created.

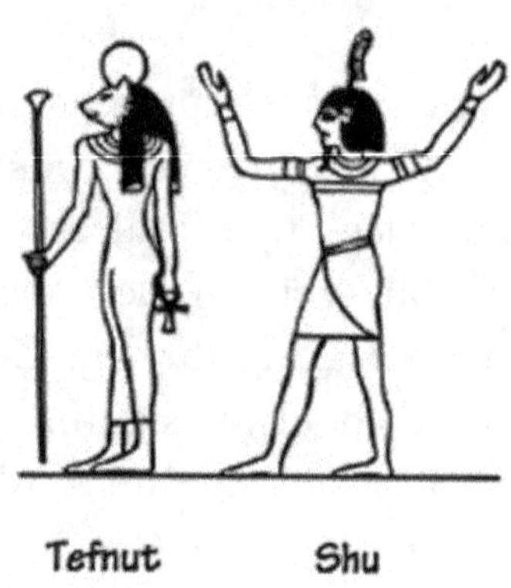

Heat (Shu) and water (Tefnut) are the two most universal shaping factors of life forms. These terms correspond to fire (heat) and moisture, respectively, and are to be understood as metaphors and actual correspondences for the abstract qualities that they represent. Shu, represented by fire, air, and heat, corresponds to the quality of expansiveness, rising, centrifugal forces, positive, masculine, outgoing, outward extroversion, etc.

Tefnut, represented by moisture and the objective material basis of manifestation (Nut, the suffix), corresponds to contraction, downward movement, centripetal forces, negative, feminine, receptive, inner, introspection, etc.

The above Ancient Egyptian concept concurs with modern scientists, who tell us that the galaxies are subjected, now, to mainly two opposing forces: 1) the expulsion forces, which cause all galaxies to move away from us; and 2) the gravitational/contractional forces, which pull the galaxies together.

6.3.A.iii Isis and Nephthys

The two female deities Isis and Nephthys appear together in numerous places in the Egyptian records. They may be considered Twin Sisters—or better yet, the dual nature of the female principle.

On the universal level, Isis represents the active expanding womb that is called the universe, and her twin sister Nephthys represents the outer limits or perimeter of the universal bubble. They both ensure an orderly enlargement and contraction of the universal bubble.

The twin sisters are mirror images of each other. Isis represents the part of the world that is visible, while Nephthys represents that which is invisible.

Isis and Nephthys respectively represent the things that are and the things that are yet to come into being—the beginning and the end—birth and death.

Isis symbolizes birth, growth, development and vigor. Nephthys represents death, decay and immobility. Nephthys is associated with the coming into existence of the life that springs from death. Isis and Nephthys are always associated inseparably with each other, and in all the important matters that concern the welfare of the deceased. They act together and they appear together in Egyptian bas-reliefs and vignettes.

This is the female dual nature, as represented by the *Twin Sisters*.

6.3.A.iv Maati

The Egyptians perceived the universe in terms of a dualism

between Ma-at—Truth and Order—and disorder. Amen-Renef summoned the cosmos out of undifferentiated chaos by distinguishing the two and by giving voice to the ultimate ideal of Truth. Ma-at, as shown here, is usually portrayed in the double form—Maati.

In the Ancient Egyptian scenes of Judgment Day, the soul of the deceased is led to the Hall of Judgment of the *Double-Ma-at*. She is double because the scale balances only when there is an equality of opposing forces. Maat's symbol is the ostrich feather, representing judgment or truth. Her feather is customarily mounted on the scales. The heart, as a metaphor for conscience, is weighed against the feather of truth to determine the fate of the deceased. [More details about this process towards the end of this book.]

6.3.A.v *Re & Thoth*

Egyptian creation texts repeatedly stress the belief of creation by the Word. When nothing existed except the One, he created the universe with his commanding voice. The Egyptian *Book of the Coming Forth by Light* (wrongly and commonly translated as the *Book of the Dead*), the oldest written text in the world, states:

> **I am the Eternal ... I am that which created the Word ... I am the Word ...**

In Ancient Egypt, the words of Re, revealed through Thoth, became the things and creatures of this world; i.e. the words (meaning sound waves) created the forms in the universe.

The word (sound) energies of Thoth transformed the creation concept/impulse of Re (symbolized in a circle) into a physical and metaphysical reality. Such transformation is reflected in the Ancient Egyptian process of **"squaring the circle"**, as evident in all their "mathematical" papyri. In all these Egyptian papyri, the area of a circle was obtained by finding the equivalent square. The diameter was always represented as 9 cubits. The Ancient Egyptian papyri equate the 9 cubit diameter circle to a square with the sides of 8 cubits.

The number 9, as the diameter, represents the Grand Ennead—the group of 9 neteru (gods, goddesses). The 9 are all aspects of Re, the primeval cosmic creative force whose symbol is/was the circle.

As will be shown later, 8 represents the manifested creation as represented by *the Master of Eight*; namely Thoth.

Musically, the ratio of 8:9 is called (appropriately enough) The Perfect Tone. Temple sanctuaries, such as the top sanctuary at the Luxor Temple, are an 8:9 rectangular shape.

6.3.A.vi *Isis & Osiris—The Dynamic Dual*

Isis and Osiris are the dynamic dual that regulates the action within the universal bubble that contains all creation.

The most significant aspects of this duality are best described by Diodorus of Sicily, who wrote in his book, *Volume I*:

> *"Isis and Osiris hold, regulate the entire universe, giving both nourishment and increase to all things..."*

[More information was shown earlier in Chapter 4, above; and additional information is given in later chapters of this book.]

6.3.A.vii *Seth and Horus & Osiris —The Power of Opposition*

The pre-creation state [as described earlier] was caused by the effect of gravitational/contractional forces that pulled and crushed atoms out of their orbits.

The act of creation was/is to bring order to the atoms by countering/opposing the crushing forces. Therefore, to the Ancient Egyptians, opposition forces were a necessity of creation and its continuance.

The neter (energy/power/force), Seth, represents the universal role of opposition.

The world as we know it—from the smallest particle to the largest planet—is kept in balance by a law that is based on the balanced dual nature of all things. Without the balance between the two opposing forces, there would be no creation; i.e., no universe.

It is therefore that Seth is not evil in the narrow sense. He represents the concept of opposition in all aspects of life (physically and metaphysically).

Unlike Christian theologians, the question of the nature and existence of Seth gave the Egyptians no trouble at all.

Horus and Seth

There are basically two forces within each of us: one pulling us down into the box, and the other pulling us out of the box. This archetypal inner struggle in the Egyptian model is symbolized in the struggle between Horus and Seth. It is the archetypal struggle between opposing forces. Horus, in this context, is the divine man, born of nature, who must do battle against Seth, his own kin, representing the power of opposition (and not evil in the narrow sense). Seth represents the concept of opposition in all aspects of life (physically and metaphysically).

We must continuously learn and evolve, like Horus—whose name means *He Who is Above*. In other words: we must strive to reach higher and higher. We learn and act by affirmation of the Horus in each of us, and by negating the Seth within us. The obstacles within each of us, represented by Seth, must be controlled and/or overcome by battling the enemies (impurities) within.

Osiris and Seth

Osiris as the Manifester of the Truth was always opposed by Seth. In the typical Ancient Egyptian story form, Plutarch writes in his *Moralia, Vol. V* (356, 13), about how Osiris was invited by Seth to a feast where Seth and his accomplices tricked Osiris into laying down in a makeshift coffin. Plutarch continues with:

> *. . . and those who were in the plot ran to it and slammed down the lid, which they fastened by nails from the outside and also by using molten lead. Then they carried the chest to the river and sent it on its way to the sea ... the Egyptians say also that the date on which this deed was done was the 17ᵗʰ day of Athor [27 November], when the sun passes through Scorpion.*

The events of 17 Hatoor/Athor (27 November), as reported by Plutarch, have all the elements of the biblical Jesus' Last Supper; i.e. a conspiracy, feast, friends, and betrayal. However, for the Ancient Egyptians, there are other meanings to the story. Plutarch, in *Moralia Vol. V* (366, 39D), wrote:

> *The story told of the shutting up of Osiris in the chest seems to mean nothing else than the vanishing and disappearance of water. . . at the time when. . . the Nile recedes to its low level and the land becomes denuded. As the nights grow longer, the*

darkness increases, and the potency of the light is abated and subdued...

The *antagonistic* relationship between Osiris and Seth—as it relates to environmental conditions—is mentioned by Plutarch, *Moralia Vol. V* (364, 33B), as such:

> *... The Egyptians simply give the name of Osiris to the whole source and faculty creative of moisture, believing this to be the cause of generation and the substance of life-producing seed; and the name of Seth they give to all that is dry, fiery, and arid, in general, and antagonistic to moisture.. ...*

> *... The insidious scheming and usurpation of Seth, then, is the power of drought, which gains control and dissipates the moisture which is the source of the Nile and of its rising.*

6.3.B UNIFICATION ASPECTS

i – The "Two Plants"
ii – Horus and Thoth
ii – Two Hapis [Unisex]
iv – Qareens of the Two Lands

6.3.B.i The "Two Plants"

Throughout Ancient Egyptian temples, you will find numerous symbolic representations that are referred to as Uniting the Two Lands, where two deities are shown tying a line of open bud with another line of closed bud. They are erroneously referred to as papyrus and lotus plants. Neither plant is native to any specific area in Egypt.

Both forms—open and closed—are found in scenes of marshes, and both forms are also shown alternating along the perimeters of nets in all eras of Egyptian history.

The closed form represents the metaphysical—hidden; unmanifested. The open form represents the physical—the manifested.

6.3.B.ii Horus and Thoth—Cosmic Faculties

One of the most visible applications of duality in Egyptian monuments is the combined action of Horus and Thoth, depicted in numerous illustrations in the Ancient Egyptian temples as performing the symbolic *Uniting of the Two Lands*.

Horus represents conscience, mind, and intellect, and is identified with the heart. Thoth represents manifestation and deliverance, and is identified with the tongue.

In the Ancient Egyptian traditions, the active faculties of Atam were intelligence, which was identified with the heart and represented as Horus—a solar neter (god) – and action, which was identified with the tongue and represented as Thoth—a lunar neter (god).

The solar and lunar neteru stresses his universal character.

In the Shabaka Stele (dated from the 8th century BCE, but is a reproduction of a 3rd Dynasty text), we read:

> **There came into being as the heart (Horus), and there came into being as the tongue (Thoth), the form of Atam.**

One thinks with the heart and acts with the tongue, as described on the Shabaka Stele:

> **The Heart thinks all that it wishes, and the Tongue delivers all that it wishes.**

6.3.B.iii Two Hapis [Unisex]

The Egyptian Pharaoh was always referred to as the *Lord of the Two Lands*. Western academia cavalierly stated that the Two Lands are *Upper and Lower Egypt*. There is not a single Ancient Egyptian reference to confirm their notion, or even to define any type of a frontier between Upper and Lower Egypt.

Throughout Ancient Egyptian temples, you will find numerous symbolic representations that are referred to as Uniting the Two Lands, where two deities are shown tying a line of open bud with another line of closed bud. They are erroneously referred to as papyrus and lotus plants. Neither plant is native to any specific area in Egypt.

By taking a closer look at Hapi, we find that Hapi appears to be a unisex deity depicted as a male figure with a female breast.

6.3.B.iv Qareens of the Two Lands

The term *Two Lands* is very familiar to the Baladi Egyptians, who refer to it in their daily life. It is their strong belief that there are *Two Lands*—the one we live on, and another one where our identical twins (of the opposite sex) live. The two are subject to the same experiences from date of birth to date of death. You and your "Siamese" twin, who "apparently" separate at birth, will reunite again at the moment of death.

The Baladi Egyptian Enumerators describe, in their lamentations after the death of a person, how the deceased is being prepared to join his/her counterpart (of the opposite sex) AS IF it is a marriage ceremony. This is reminiscent of the many symbolic illustrations in Ancient Egypt of the tying the knot of the Two Lands. To be married is to tie the knot.

In the Egyptian common language, the word Qareen means "a spouse".

As far back as the Unas (so-called "Pyramid") Texts, one finds that the Pharaoh Unas (2356–2323 BCE) unites/ joins with Isis immediately after departing the earthly realm. This is based on the premise that since every man is Osiris in his "dead" form, each joins his/her counterpart (Isis, in the case of a man) at the moment of earthly departure.

6.3.C CYCLICAL ASPECTS

i – Osiris and Horus
ii – Re and Osiris

6.3-C.i *Osiris and Horus*

Father 'and' Son

In the Egyptian allegory, Osiris' wife Isis was able to conceive her child Horus without Osiris' impregnation. It was the first recorded immaculate conception in history.

The Egyptians looked at Osiris and Horus as One, in two complimentary forms.

The interchangeable relationship between the Father and the Son is eloquently illustrated here, where Horus is being born out of Osiris, after Osiris' death, with the solar disk rising with the newborn.

This concept is translated into the common expression

"The King is dead. Long live the King."

As if to say, *"Osiris is dead. Long live Horus".*

Neither Osiris nor Horus were ever regarded as historical.

Osiris represents the mortal man carrying within himself the capacity and power of spiritual salvation.

Osiris symbolizes the subconscious—the capacity to act; to do – while Horus symbolizes consciousness, will, and the potential to act; to do.

On Judgment Day, Horus, son of Isis, acts as a mediator between the deceased and The Father Osiris. All Egyptians wanted/want The Son of God Horus to bring them

(dead) to life, as depicted in these Egyptian tombs.

The Water Cycle of Osiris and Horus

The duality of Osiris and Horus are reflected in the water cycle as represented in the four universal four elements Water, Air, Fire and Earth

The four elements of the world (water, fire, earth, and air), as quoted from Plutarch's *Moralia Vol. V, are:*

> **The Egyptians simply give the name of Osiris to the whole source and faculty creative of moisture, believing this to be the cause of generation and the substance of life-producing seed; and the name of Seth they give to all that is dry, fiery, and arid, in general, and antagonistic to moisture. As the Egyptians regard the Nile as the effusion of Osirs, so they hold and believe the earth to be the body of Isis, not all of it, but so much of it as the Nile covers, fertilizing it and uniting with it. From this union they make Horus to be born. The all conserving and fostering Hora, that is the seasonable tempering of the surrounding air, is Horus The insidious scheming and usurpation of Seth, then, is the power of drought, which gains control and dissipates the moisture which is the source of the Nile and of its rising.**

Here we see how the water cycle is represented in a story form.

The original water is Osiris—which due to the heat of Seth causes the water to evaporate into the air [being Horus].

Later, in due time, the rising water vapor of Horus will return by condensation in the form of water—being Osiris. And on and on

…

And on and on …

6.3.C.ii Re and Osiris

Egyptian texts refer to Re and Osiris as the *Twin Souls.*

Etymologically, the relationship between Re/Ra and Osiris becomes self evident. The Egyptian word for Osiris is Aus-Ra.

The word Aus means *the power of,* or *the root of.* As such, the name Ausar consists of two parts: Aus-Ra, meaning *the power of Ra,* meaning the *re-birth of Ra.*

The perpetual cycle of existence—the cycle of life and death—is symbolized by Ra (Re) and Ausar (Osiris). Ra is the living neter who descends into death to become Ausar, the neter of the dead. Ausar ascends and comes to life again as Ra. The creation is continuous: it is a flow of life progressing towards death. But out of death, a new Ra is to be born, sprouting new life. Ra is the cosmic principle of energy that moves toward death, and Ausar represents the process of rebirth. Thus, the terms of life and death become interchangeable: life means slow dying, and death means resurrection to new life. The dead person in death is identified with Ausar, but he will come to life again and will be identified with Ra.

The perpetual cycle of Ausar and Ra dominates the Ancient Egyptian texts, such as:

- In *The Book of the Coming Forth By Light*, both Ausar and Ra live, die, and are born again. In the Netherworld, the souls of Ausar and Ra meet [see illustration from the Papyrus of Ani, below] and are united to form an entity, described so eloquently:

  I am His Two Souls in his Twins.

In Chapter 17 of *The Book of the Coming Forth By Light*, the deceased, identified with Ausar, says:

> *I am yesterday, I know the morrow.*

- And the Egyptian commentary to this passage explains:

> *What is this?—Ausar is yesterday, Ra is tomorrow?*

- In the tomb of Queen Nefertari (wife of Ramses II) is a well-known representation of the dead solar neter (god) as a mummiform body with the head of a ram, accompanied by an inscription, right and left:

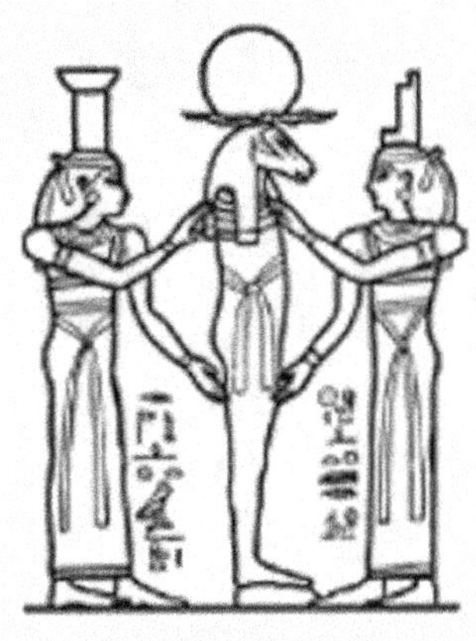

This is Ra who comes to rest in Ausar.

This is Ausar who comes to rest in Ra.

- The Litany of Re is basically a detailed amplification of a short passage of Chapter 17 of The *Book of the Coming Forth by Light*, describing the merging of Ausar and Ra into a *Twin Soul*.

Chapter 7 : Three—The United Trinity

7.1 THE FIRST ODD NUMBER

As stated earlier, Plutarch noted that One, for the Egyptians, was not an (odd) number when he wrote: *three is the first perfect odd number*. For the Egyptians, one was not a number, but the essence of the underlying principle of number; all other numbers being made of it. One represents Unity: the Absolute as unpolarized energy. One is neither odd nor even, but both; because if it's added to an odd number, it makes it even, and vice-versa. So it combines the opposites of odd and even and all the other opposites in the universe. Unity is a perfect, eternal, undifferentiated consciousness.

7.2 THE THREE-IN-ONE

As we have seen in chapter 5 of this book, it takes three components to create and bring something to life. The Egyptian texts show us that Unity, becoming conscious of itself, creates polarized energy: two new elements, each of which share in the nature of the One and of the Other—being mirror images of each other.

It is the expression of the outgoing energy of the Divinity. Such is eloquently expressed in the Ancient Egyptian text known as the *Bremner-Rhind Papyrus*:

> *I was anterior to the Two Anteriors that I made,*
> *for I had priority over the Two Anteriors that I made,*

for my name was anterior to theirs,
for I made them anterior to the Two Anteriors...

So the prototype of generation encompasses three elements of the Creator Trinity.

The Ancient Egyptians recognized the significance of trinity in the creation process. As such, Ancient Egyptian texts rendered the trinity as a unity expressed by the singular pronoun—it is the Three that are Two that are One.

The principles of creation are unity ,duality and trinity. This is made clear in the Ancient Egyptian papyrus known as the *Bremner-Rhind Papyrus:*

"After having become one neter (god), there were [now]three neteru (gods, godesses) **in me. ..”**—referring to the triad of Atam and the dual Shu-and Tefnut.

The various trinities are related to various nature of the duality within each trinity. Earlier in chapter 5 of this book, the manifesting Trinity was shown to be Atam-Isis-Osiris.

7.3 OTHER TRINITY APPLICATIONS IN EGYPT

The Ancient Egyptians realized the physical and metaphysical role of Trinity; for each unity has a triple power and a double nature. A few examples of the Egyptians' implementation of this realization are:

1 – The creation cycle consists of 3 phases—Conceptual, Manifestation and Return to the Source.

2 – Stanza 300 of the Ancient Egyptian's Leiden Papyrus J350 declares the unity in one Being of the three principles, Amen, Re, and Ptah. Stanza 300 reads in part:

Three are all the neteru: Amen, Re, and Ptah. His hidden name is Amen. Re belongs to him as his face, Ptah is his body."

A stunning example of a 'Holy Trinity'.

3 – The triple shrine is the main feature in Egyptian temples, to enshrine the triple power (three neteru) of each temple.

4 – For the Ancient Egyptians, Three/Triads/Trinities/Triangles are one and the same. There was no functional difference between geometric triangles, musical triads, or any of the many trinities of Ancient Egypt. The clearest example was explained by Plutarch regarding the 3:4:5 triangle, in *Moralia Vol. V*:

> ***The Egyptians hold in high honor the most beautiful of the triangles, since they liken the nature of the Universe most closely to it...***

In other words, triangles/triads in their different forms represent different natures in the universe.

5 – The Egyptian calendar is divided into 3 (not 4) seasons, to correspond to the fluctuation of the River Nile's flow. The Nile is regarded as the effusion of Osiris [as reported by Plutarch, in his *Moralia, Vol. V*].

6 – In the Ancient Egyptian numerology, Osiris represents the number 3.

Four is the number signifying solidity and stability. A special property of four is that it is the first perfect square because it is the product of two multiplied by itself, and any number which is multiplied by itself is a (square) root and the product is a perfect square.The significance of the number 4 is shown in the following examples from Ancient Egypt:

1. Egyptian texts state that the pre-creation chaos possessed characteristics that were identified with four pairs of primordial powers/forces. Each pair represents the primeval dual-gendered twins—the masculine/feminine aspect. The four pairs are equivalent to the four forces of the universe (the weak force, the strong force, gravity, and electromagnetism).

2. Ancient Egyptians had four main cosmological teaching centers at Heliopolis, Memphis, Thebes, and Khmunu (Hermopolis). Each center revealed one of the principle phases or aspects of genesis.

Egypt now has 4 Sufi Teaching Ways, which were created in the 11th century CE, to maintain the Ancient Egyptian traditions under the Islamic rule.

3. Egyptians used the four simple phenomena (fire, air, earth and water) to describe the functional roles of the four elements necessary to matter. Water is the sum— the composite principle of fire, earth and air. Water is also a substance over and above them.

These concepts were expressed in the Ancient Egyptian texts as Nu/Nun, the primeval (liquid) water that contains all elements of the universe. Plutarch confirmed that about Ancient Egyptians, in his *Moralia Vol. V*:

> **For the nature of water, being the source and origin of all things, created out of itself three primal material substances: Earth, Air, and Fire.**

The four elements of the world (water, fire, earth, and air), as quoted from Plutarch's *Moralia Vol. V*, are:

> **The Egyptians simply give the name of Osiris to the whole source and faculty creative of moisture, believing this to be the cause of generation and the substance of life-producing seed; and the name of Seth they give to all that is dry, fiery, and arid, in general, and antagonistic to moisture. As the Egyptians regard the Nile as the effusion of Osiris, so they hold and believe the earth to be the body of Isis, not all of it, but so much of it as the Nile covers, fertilizing it and uniting with it. From this union they make Horus to be born. The all-conserving and fostering Hora, that is the seasonable tempering of the surrounding air, is Horus. The insidious scheming and usurpation of Seth, then, is the power of drought, which gains control and dissipates the moisture which is the source of the Nile and of its rising.**

4. Stanza 40 of the Ancient Egyptians' Leiden Papyrus J350 introduces the 'Becoming', telling of the Divine Craftsman of the universe symbolized as Ptah, *The Manifester of Forms*.

In Ancient Egypt, Ptah was the cosmic shaping force; the giver of form (smith). He was the coagulating, creative fire; simultaneously the cause (of the created world) and effect (of the scission).

Ptah's main cosmological center was at Memphis, which was one of the four main cosmological centers in Ancient Egypt.

5. The Tet (Djed) pillar, symbol of the support of creation, has four elements.

6. Other applications are: the four children of the neter (god) Geb (representing the universal material/physical aspect), the 4 cardinal points, the 4 regions of the sky, the 4 pillars of the sky (material support of the realm of the spirit), the 4 disciples (sons) of Horus, and the 4 canopic jars into which the 4 organs were placed after death.

Chapter 9 : The Fifth Star

The significance and function of number five, in Ancient Egypt, is indicated by the manner in which it was written. The number 5 in Ancient Egypt was written as 2 (II) above 3 (III), or as a five-pointed star. In other words: number 5 is the result of the relationship between number 2 and number 3.

Two symbolizes the power of multiplicity – the female, mutable receptacle – while Three symbolizes the male. This was the 'music of the spheres'; the universal harmonies played out between these two primal male and female universal symbols of Osiris and Isis, whose heavenly marriage produced the child Horus.

Plutarch confirmed this Egyptian wisdom in *Moralia Vol. V*:

Three [Osiris] is the first perfect odd number: four is a square whose side is the even number two [Isis]; but five [Horus] is in some ways like to its father, and in some ways like to its mother, being made up of three and two. And panta (all) is a derivative of pente (five), and they speak of counting as "numbering by fives".

Five incorporates the principles of polarity (II) and reconciliation (III). All phenomena, without exception, are polar in nature and treble in principle. Therefore, five is the key to understanding the manifested universe, as per Plutarch on the Egyptian thinking:

...And panta (all) is a derivative of pente (five).

Five is the building block in the creation process.

The number 'five' is considered the most important number in mathematics, philosophy, and music. [More details in other publications by same author.]

Every number has one or more special properties; meaning the particular qualities of the described object which nothing shares with it. A special property of five is that it is the first recurrent number, also called 'spherical'.

Five is the first recurrent number because when it is multiplied by itself, it returns to itself; and if that number is multiplied by itself, it again returns to its essence, and so on forever. So, for example, five times five is twenty-five , and if this number is multiplied by itself, the product is six hundred and twenty-five, and if this number is again multiplied by itself, the product is 390.625, and if this number is multiplied by itself, the product is another number ending in twenty-five. Five conserves itself and whatever derives from it eternally; whatever it may reach.

Five may also be called the first 'universal' number. Five accounts for 'creation'. It is that which conceives, quickens, develops and brings forth all things perceived and set forth by The Holy Spirit.

9.2 THE FIVE PHASES OF HORUS

Horus is the personification of the goal of all initiated teachings, and therefore is associated with the number five; for he is the fifth, after Isis, Osiris, Seth and Nephthys. Horus is also the number 5 in the right angle triangle of 3:4:5, as confirmed by Plutarch.

Horus declares, in *The Egyptian Book of Coming Forth by Light* (incorrectly known as *The Egyptian Book of the Dead*) [c. 78]:

> **"I am Horus in glory"; "I am the Lord of Light"; "I am the victorious one . . . I am the heir of endless time"; "I am he that knoweth the paths of heaven."**

The above Ancient Egyptian verses were echoed later in Jesus' words, *"I am the light of the world,"* and again, *"I am the way, the truth and the life."*

Horus, in the Ancient Egyptian language, means *He who is above*. As such, Horus represents the realized divine principle. Horus is the personification of the goal of all initiated teachings, who is always depicted accompanying the realized soul to the Source.

As the model of earthly existence, Horus is represented in several forms and aspects to correspond with the stages in the process of spiritualization.

The five most common forms of Horus are:

1. Hor-Sa-Auset, which means Horus, Son of Isis. Horsiesis (or Harsiesis) is often shown as an infant being suckled by Isis, which is identical to the later Christian representation of the Madonna and her child. In the lifespan of a person, this is the age of total dependency.

2. Heru-p-Khart/Hor-Pa-Khred, which means Horus the Child [Harpocrates]. He is often shown with his forefinger on his mouth, symbolizing the taking in of knowledge. This is the age of learning, with an inquisitive mind.

3. Horus Behdetyor [Apollo] is Horus who avenged the death of his father and flew up to heaven in the form of a winged disk. This represents the stage in our life of working and struggling to achieve higher spiritual realms, so that one can

fly up to heaven, victorious. Depictions of Horus Behdety are found in most Ancient Egyptian structures; but more prominently at the Edfu Temple.

4. Heru-ur, which means Horus the Elder or Horus the Great or Haroeris/Harueris. He is usually depicted as a hawk-headed male divinity wearing the double crown. This represents the stage of reaching the age of wisdom (hence the title, Horus the Elder). Horus The Elder is depicted in numerous Ancient Egyptian temples, but more prominently at Kom Ombo.

5. Hor-Akhti/Horachty [Harmachis], which means Horus on/of the Horizon—a form of a new morning sun. Hor-Akhti signifies the renewal/new beginning; a new day. This will be manifested in the form of ReHor.Akhti.

9.3 THE DESTINY—FIVE POINTED STAR

Stanzas 50 and 500 of the Ancient Egyptian Leiden Papyrus J350, whose first word *dua* means, at the same time, *five* and to *worship*, consist of hymns of adoration exalting the marvels of Creation.

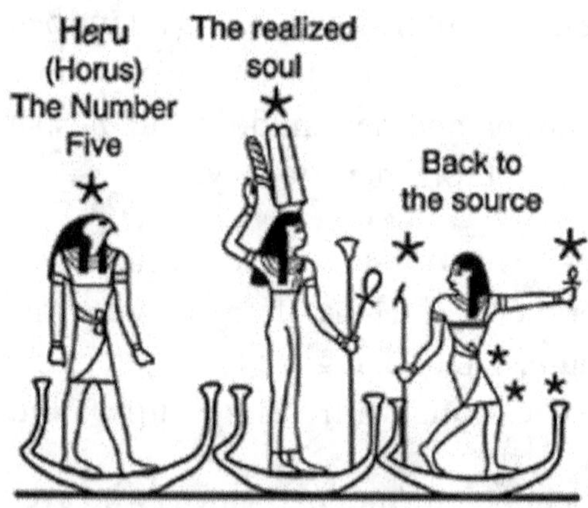

In Ancient Egypt, the symbol for a star was drawn with five points. The Star was the Egyptian symbol for both destiny and the number five.

The Egyptian five-pointed star forms the corners of the pentagon, which is harmoniously inscribed in the Sacred Circle of Re. The Star was the Egyptian symbol for both destiny and the number five.

The five-pointed stars are the homes of the successfully departed souls, as stated in the *Unas Funerary Texts* (known as *Pyramid Texts*), Line 904:

be a soul as a living star ...

Egyptian 5-pointed stars are found all over ancient Egyptian tombs and temples, throughout its history.

Chapter 10 : The Cubical Sixth

In the previous chapter, we found that five terms are needed to account for 'creation'. Six provides the framework for the actualization of potentiality. That framework is time and space. We may call Six the number of the world, in this sense. Five, in becoming Six, engenders or creates time and space.

A special property of the number six is that it is the first perfect number; i.e., if the divisors of a number add up to itself, it is called a perfect number, and six is the first of them. Six has a half which is three, and a third which is two, and a sixth which is one; and if these divisors are added up, the sum is equal to six.

The number 6 is not self-continuing, as five is. Its prolongation is 6 36 1296. Six times six is thirty-six; six returns to itself, and thirty appears. When thirty-six is multiplied by itself, the product is 1296 – six again appears; but not thirty. So it is evident that six conserves itself, but not what is derived from it. But five conserves itself and what derives from it eternally and forever.

Six is the cosmic number of the material world and therefore is the number chosen by the Egyptians to symbolize both time and space. Time and space are two sides of the same coin, which is perfectly represented in the science of astronomy and its application, astrology. Scientists now agree that there is a very close connection between space and time—so close that you can't have one without the other.

1. Time – Anything to do with timekeeping, for the Ancient

Egyptians, was and is based on the number six, or its multiples. The whole day was/is 24 (6 x 4) hours, consisting of 12 (6 x 2) hours of daytime and 12 (6 x 2) hours of nighttime. The hour was/is 60 (6 x 10) minutes, and the minute was/is 60 seconds. The month was/is 30 days (6 x 5). The year was/is 12 months (6 x 2). The Great Zodiac Year contained 12 Zodiac Ages (signs).

2. Space (Volume) – requires 6 directions of extension to define it: up and down, backwards and forwards, and left and right. The cube, the perfect 6-sided figure, was used in Egypt as the symbol for space (volume).

The Egyptian was highly conscious of the box-like structure, which is the model of the earth or the material world. The forms of statuary called the "cube statue" are prevalent since the Middle Kingdom (2040-1783 BCE). The subject was integrated into the cubic form of the stone. In these cube statues, there is a powerful sense of the subject emerging from the prison of the cube. Its symbolic significance is that the spiritual principle is emerging from the material world. The earthly person is placed unmistakably in material existence.

The Divine person is shown sitting squarely on a cube i.e. mind over matter.

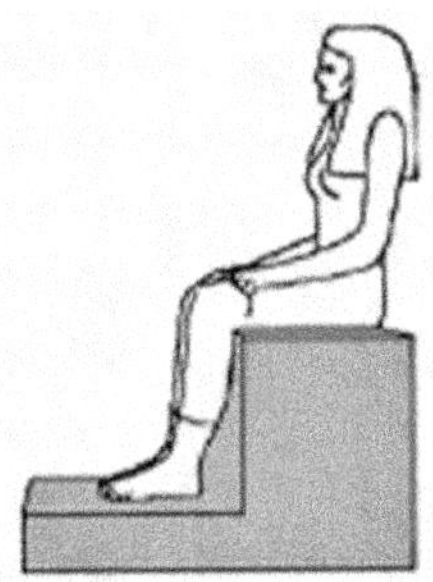

Other traditions, such as the Platonic and Pythagorean, adopted the same concept of the Egyptian cubic representation of the material world.

Chapter 11 : The Cyclical Seven

The universe is constructed in accordance with the nature of numbers. The number seven is the first complete number because seven combines in itself the meanings of all the (preceding) numbers. For all the numbers are even or odd, two is the first even number, and four is the second; three is the first odd number and five is the second. If the first odd number is added to the second even number, or the first even number is added to the second odd number, the sum is seven. So, if you add two, the first even number, to five, the second odd number, the sum is seven; similarly, if you add three (which is the first odd number) to four (which is the second even number), the sum is seven. And if one, which is the source of all numbers, is taken with six, which is a perfect number, the sum is seven, which is a complete number. This is their table: 1 2 3 4 5 6 7. This is a special property of seven which no other number before seven possesses.

The numbers 7, 9, 12, 28 are the first numbers that are called complete (kamil), odd square, exceeding and perfect respectively. Also, the cause of the exclusivity of those numbers comes, on the one hand, from the fact that 7 = 3 + 4; 12 = 3 x 4; 28 = 7 x 4; and on the other hand, 7 + 12 + 9 = 28.

The mystical function of the number 7 in Ancient Egypt is signified as the union of spirit (Three) and matter (Four). One of the forms that traditionally expresses the meaning of 7 is the pyramid, which combines the square base symbolizing the four elements and the triangular sides symbolizing the three modes of spirit.

Esoterically, because all numbers are to be regarded as divisions of unity, the mathematical relationship a number bears to unity is a key to its nature. Both three and seven are 'perpetual motion' numbers. Divided into unity, they divide infinitely:

$$1/3 = .33333...$$
$$1/7 = .14285714285714...$$

Seven is the number of process, growth, and the underlying cyclical aspects of the universe. Osiris represents the same exact principles; and as such, he is associated with the number 7 and its multiples.

Seven of something frequently makes a complete set—the 7 days of the week, 7 colors of the spectrum, 7 notes of the musical scale, etc. The cells of the human body are totally renewed every 7 years.

The intimate relationship between Osiris and 7 is reflected in these few examples from the Temple of Osiris at Abydos:

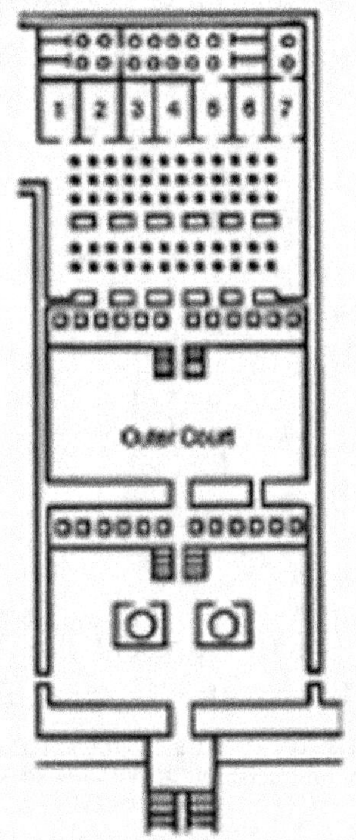

1. It is the only temple that has 7 chapels.

2. There are 7 spirit forms of Osiris.

3. There are 7 boats of Osiris.

4. 42 (7 x 6) is the number of assessors/jurors on Judgment Day, where Osiris presides.

5. 42 (7 x 6) is the number of steps leading to this temple.

• • •

The Tet (Djed) pillar, as the sacred symbol of Osiris, has 7 steps. This is reminiscent of the doctrine of chakras in the Indian kundalini system of yoga, which is much younger than the Ancient Egyptian traditions. The chakras are centers in the psychophysical structure of man that accord with the 7 constituents of man, along with the link that draws them together; namely, the human backbone.

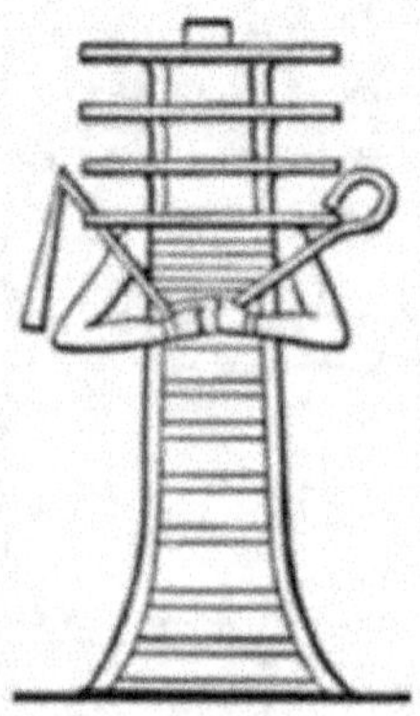

The 7 centers of Tet (Djed) represent the 7 metaphorical rungs of the ladder leading from matter to spirit. Since man is a microcosm of the cosmic pattern, Tet represents a microcosm of the universal cosmology.

It is hard to separate the number 7 from Osiris. The principle that makes life come from apparent death was/is called Osiris, who symbolizes the power of renewal. Osiris represents the process, growth, and the underlying cyclical aspects of the universe. Therefore, he was also identified with the spirits (energies) of grain, trees, animals, reptiles, birds, etc.

The most impressive representation of the concept of regeneration, namely Osiris, is the illustration depicting Osiris with 28 stalks of wheat growing out of his coffin. It is also interesting to note that Osiris' life (or his reign), according to the symbolic Egyptian Model Story, lasted 28 (7 x 4) years.

("The Resurrection of the Wheat")

Osiris' cyclical nature made him relate to the number 7 and its multiples. Very often, we find that seven or multiples of seven are needed to account for the principle and sequence of growth. Throughout the entire world, menstruation appears to be connected with the moon; the courses of the moon being likened to the courses of a woman. The moon is thus the appropriate symbol of fertility. As he waxes and wanes, he is regarded as a dying and resurrecting cycle—the symbol of the death and rebirth of the crops. Menstruation in women, on which all human life depends, occurs in a cycle of 28 (7 x 4) days.

Osiris is identified with the moon, as explained earlier.

Osiris died (analogous to the moon's departure) and was resurrected the third day after that. The third day is the beginning of a new moon; i.e., a renewed Osiris. This is reminiscent of the Easter celebration where, like Osiris, the biblical Jesus died on Friday and was resurrected the third day—Sunday—as a new life.

Chapter 12 : Eight, The Octave

Seven is the end of a cycle. Eight is the beginning of a new cycle—an octave.

As shown in this book, Ancient and Baladi Egyptians believe that the universe consists of 9 realms (7 heavens and 2 lands/earths). Our earthly existence is the 8th realm (first land/earth).

At number 8, we find the human being created in the image of God, the First Principle. Our earthly existence at the 8th realm is a replication and not a duplication—an octave. 'Octave' is the future state of the past. The continuance of creation is a series of replications—octaves. Eight, then, corresponds to the manifested physical world as we experience it.

In Egypt, the well-known text *Coffin of Petamon* [Cairo Museum item no. 1160] states:

> *I am One who becomes Two,*
> *who becomes Four,*
> *who becomes Eight,*
> *and then I am One again.*

This new unity (One again) is not identical, but is analogous to the first unity (I am One). The old unity is no longer; a new unity has taken its place – *The King is Dead, Long Live the King.* It is a renewal or self-replication. And to account for the principle of self-replication, 8 terms are necessary.

Musically, the renewal theme of 8 terms corresponds to the octave because it reaches through all 8 intervals of the scale (the 8 white keys of the keyboard).

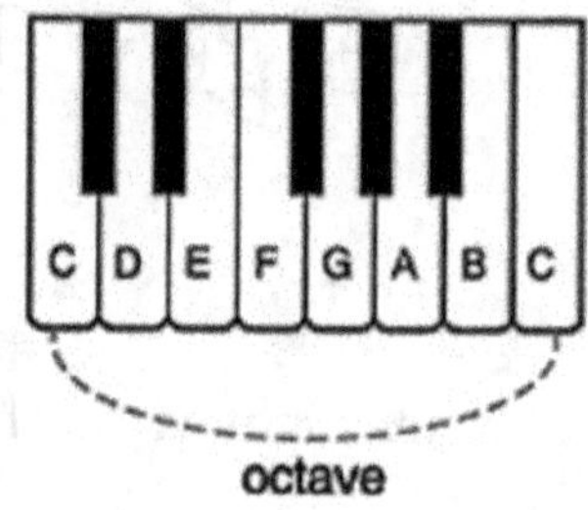

For example, an octave can be 2 successive Cs (Do's) on a musical scale, as illustrated above on the keyboard.

– Eight is written as IIII over IIII.

– Eight is the number of Thoth, and at Khmunu (Hermopolis), Thoth is called the **Master of the City of Eight.**

Thoth was the messenger of the neteru (gods, goddesses) of writing, and of language, of knowledge. Thoth gave man access to the mysteries of the manifested world, which were symbolized by the number Eight.

Stanza 80 of the Ancient Egyptian Leiden Papyrus J350 retraces the Creation as told in Khmunu (Hermopolis), which deals with the Ogdoad—the Primordial Eight—which comprised the first metamorphosis of Amen-Re, the mysterious, hidden one who is recognized as Ta-Tenen at Memphis, then Ka-Mut-f at Thebes; yet all the while remaining One.

Therefore, the manifestation of creation in 8 terms are present in all four Ancient Egyptian cosmological centers:

- At Memphis, Ptah, in his 8 forms, he created the universe.

- At Heliopolis, Atam created the 8 divine beings.

- At Khmunu (Hermopolis), 8 primeval neteru—the Ogdoad—created the universe. They were the representation of the primeval state of the universe.

- At Thebes, Amun/Aman/Amen after creating himself in secret, created the Ogdoad.

The manifestation of creation through 8 terms is also reflected in the mystical process of squaring the circle. [See the details earlier regarding the subject of the Re and Thoth duality.]

Chapter 13 : The Nine Lives

13.1 THE UNIVERSAL SIGNIFICANCE OF THE NUMBER NINE

Number nine marks the end of gestation and the end of each series of numbers. If multiplied by any other number, it always reproduces itself (3 x 9 = 27 and 2 + 7 = 9 or 6 x 9 = 54 and 5 + 4 = 9. and so on).

Nine marks the transition from one scale (the numbers from 1 to 9) to a higher scale (starting with 10), and so it is the number of initiation, which is again similar to the birth of a baby after nine months.

A human child is normally conceived, formed, and born in nine months; a fact which has a good deal to do with the role and importance attached to the number nine in Ancient Egypt.

Correspondingly, the Ancient Egyptian refers to a group of nine divinities as one unit—being an Ennead. As stated earlier, we find that, as far back as at least 5000 years ago, the Pyramid Texts reveal the existence of three companies of neteru (gods, goddesses), and each company consisted of 9 neteru (gods, goddesses).

The Egyptian texts speak of three Enneads, each representing a phase in the creation cycle, as explained earlier.

The nine aspects of an Ennead are not a sequence, but a unity—interpenetrating, interacting, and interlocked.

Number 9 marks the end of gestation and the end of each series of numbers.

In the *Litany of Re*, Re is described as *The One of the Cat*, and as *The Great Cat*. The nine realms of the universe are manifested in the cat; for both the cat and the Grand Ennead (meaning nine-times-unity) have the same Ancient Egyptian term b.st. This relationship has found its way to Western culture, where one says that *the cat has nine lives* (realms).

13.2 THE NINE TIERS OF THE UNIVERSAL MATRIX

Since the created universe is orderly, its energy matrix is likewise a well-oiled machine with nine interpenetrating and interacting realms.

Ancient and Baladi Egyptians believe that the universal energy matrix consists of nine realms which are commonly classified as seven heavens (metaphysical realms) and two Earths (physical realms).

The two earthly realms are commonly known as *The Two Lands*. In the previous chapter, we followed the significance of the number 8, as our physical (earthly) realm.

The last realm—number 9—is where our complimentary opposite exists. The Siamese twins who live in realms 8 and 9 are in perfect harmony. In musical terms, the ratio/ relationship 8:9 represents the Perfect Tone.

The concept of 9 realms is consistent with the concept of the Grand Ennead—the unity of 9; the generator of the manifested creation.

The energies in the 9 realms form an orderly interactive hierarchy. [Interacting between energies is shown in later chapters.]

13.3 THE NINE TIERS OF MAN

Just as our lives do not stop at death, so our bodies are not limited by their outer physical forms. We exist on a number of different levels at once, from the most physical to the most spiritual. Indeed, in one sense, there is no difference between physical and spiritual; only the gradations that lie between the two ends of the spectrum.

The whole man consisted of:

1. A vital force—Sekhem
Sekhem is the vital power.

Re is called *The Great Sekhem.*

2. A name—Ren
Ren as a "name" is the essence of an individual which distinguishes one person from another. When your name is called, you return to the Source.

3. A Spirit-soul—Khu
The khu is a higher spiritual element. It is a shining and luminous component. Khus are also heavenly beings, living with the neteru (gods, goddesses). Each khu may then be equivalent to the guardian angel.

4. A shadow—Khaibet
The khaibit seems to correspond with our notion of the ghost.

Khai = companion/brother

5. A Heart-soul—Ba
Ba represents totality of man's physical and psychic capacities.

The Ba is immortal. When the ba departs, the body dies.

The Ba is represented as a human-headed bird, as the divine aspect of the terrestrial.

6. A double—Ka
The Ka is the combination of several intertwined sub-components. It is equated to what we describe as personality. The Ka does not die with the mortal body, although it may break into its many sub-components.

7. A heart—Ab
The heart is the seat of power, consciousness, and right and wrong.

Horus is called "dweller in hearts" or "lord of hearts."

Ab [as the heart] is the reverse spelling of the component Ba—the heart-soul.

8. A Spirit-body—Sahu
A metaphysical body that leaves the physical body with proper funerary rights has the power to travel anywhere lasting and incorruptible.

Sahu is shown as a mummy lying on a bier, indicating a spirit body that is lasting and incorruptible.

Ab is reverse for Ba = heart-soul

9. A natural body—Khat
Khat means corruptible—subject to decay.

More details about the nine components will be shown in a later chapter of this book.

Chapter 14 : Ten, a New One

In ancient Egypt, the number 10 symbolized completion and perfection because it completed the series of the essential numbers and brought them back to unity. In Egyptian philosophy, the process was symbolized by Horus, the Divine Son.

As the son of Isis and Osiris, Horus was the tenth neter (god) of the Grand Ennead.

Ten is the highest number of the original unity.

The Grand Ennead emanates from the Absolute. The nine neteru (principles) circumscribed about One (The Absolute) becomes both One and Ten. This is the symbolic analog of the original Unity; it is repetition, the return to the source.

Ten is the first number of the tens' rank, as one is the first number of the units' rank. It has another special property similar to a property of the number one; namely, that it only has one number adjacent to it, twenty; and ten is half of it—similar to the case of one which is half of two.

The logarithm of 10 is One.

Ten is a new One (log 10 = 1)

PART IV : AS ABOVE SO BELOW

Chapter 15 : The Human Being—The Universal Replica

15.1 THE ONE JOINED TOGETHER

If man is the universe in miniature, then all factors in man are duplicated on a greater scale in the universe. All drives and forces, which are powerful in man, are also powerful in the universe at large. In accordance with the Egyptians' cosmic consciousness, every action performed by man is believed to be linked to a greater pattern in the universe, including sneezing, blinking, spitting, shouting, weeping, dancing, playing, eating, drinking, and sexual intercourse.

For Ancient Egyptians, man, as a miniature universe, represents the created image of all creation. Since Re—the cosmic creative impulse—is called:

> *The One Joined together, Who Comes Out of His Own Members,*

so the human being (the image of creation) is likewise, *A One Joined Together*. The human body is a unity that consists of different parts, joined together. In the *Litany of Re*, the body parts of the divine man are each identified with a neter (god) or a netert (goddess).

Man, to the Ancient Egyptians, was the embodiment of the laws of creation. As such, the physiological functions and processes of the various parts of the body were seen as manifestations of cosmic functions. The limbs and organs had a metaphysical function, in addition to their physical purpose. The parts of the body were consecrated to one of the neteru (divine principles), which appeared in the Egyptian records throughout its recovered history. In addition to the *Litany of Re*, here are other examples:

- Utterance 215 § 148-149, from the Sarcophagus Chamber of Unas' Tomb (rubble pyramid) at Saqqara, identifies the parts of the body (head, nose, teeth, arms, legs, etc.), each with the divine neteru (gods, goddesses):

  > *Thy head is that of Horus*
  >
  > *. . .*
  >
  > *thy nose is Anubis*
  > *thy teeth are Sopdu*
  > *thy arms are Hapy and Dua-mutef,*
  >
  > *. . .*
  >
  > *thy legs are Imesty and Kebeh-senuf,*
  >
  > *. . .*
  >
  > *All thy members are the twins of Atam.*

- From the Papyrus of Ani, [pl. 32, item 42]:

  > *My hair is Nun; my face is Re; my eyes are Hathor; my ears are Wep-wawet; my nose is She who presides over her lotus-leaf; my lips are Anubis; my molars are Selket; my incisors are Isis; my arms are the Ram, the Lord of Mendes; my breast is Neith; my back is Seth; my phallus is Osiris; . . . my belly and my spine are Sekhmet; my buttocks are the Eye of Horus; my thighs and my calves are Nut; my feet are Ptah; . . . there is no member of mine devoid of a neter (god), and Thoth is the protection of all my flesh.*

The above text leaves no doubt about the divinity of each member:

15.2 METAPHYSICAL/PHYSICAL FUNCTIONS OF THE BODY PARTS

It is a human instinct worldwide to use a human organ/part to describe a metaphysical aspect. The Ancient Egyptian texts and symbols are permeated with this complete understanding that the man (whole and parts) is the image of the universe (in whole and part).

Here are a few examples in Ancient Egypt of the metaphysical/physical functions of some human parts:

• The Heart

The heart was/is considered to be a symbol of intellectual perceptions, consciousness, and moral courage. The heart is symbolized by Horus.

• The Tongue

The tongue is the strongest muscle in the human body. A man of his word means whatever he commands with his tongue will be manifested. The tongue is symbolized by Thoth.

• Both the heart and tongue complement each other, as stated clearly in the Shabaka Stele (716–701 BCE), which is a reproduction from the 3rd Dynasty:

> *the Heart thinks all that it wishes, and the Tongue delivers all that it wishes.*

[More about the roles of the heart and tongue throughout the book.]

• The Spine and Belly

In our modern societies, the guts and spine are symbols of physical courage. This concept has Ancient Egyptian roots. In the *Papyrus of Ani* [pl.32 item 42], we read,

my belly and my spine are Sekhmet

Sekhmet is a lioness-headed netert (goddess). The lioness is the most fearless animal.

[The metaphysical functions of some other human parts are described throughout the book.]

15.3 THE NINE COMPONENTS OF MAN

We exist on a number of different levels at once, from the most physical to the most spiritual. Indeed, in one sense there is no difference between physical and spiritual; only the gradations that lie between the two ends of the spectrum.

It was believed that, upon birth, a human being possessed a physical body (Khat) and an immaterial double (Ka), which lived inside the body and was associated closely with the Ba, which dwelt in the heart, and which appears to have been connected with the shadow of the physical body. Somewhere in the body lived the Khu or Spiritsoul; the nature of which was unchangeable, incorruptible, and immortal.

All these were, however, bound together inseparably, and the welfare of any single one of them concerned the welfare of all; and as far back as in the Unas (commonly known as "Pyramid") Texts they are welded together. Each has its own distinction and powers; but there are bi-lateral and tri-lateral relationships between the individual components.

In the Ancient Egyptian cosmology, the whole man consists of nine components as follows:

1. a vital force—called Sekhem
2. a [secret] name—called Ren

3. a Spirit-soul—called Khu
4. a shadow—called Khaibet
5. a Heart-soul [etheric body]—called Ba
6. a double/image—called Ka
7. a heart [conscience]—called Ab
8. a Spirit-body—called Sahu
9. a natural body—called Khat

1. Sekhem

Sekhem represents the vital power.

Re is called *the Great Sekhem*.

Sekhem is mentioned in conjunction with Ba and khu.

The Sekhem is related to [associated with] the Khu.

2. Ren

Ren, as the [secret] name of a man was believed to exist in heaven, and in the Unas ("Pyramid") Texts we are told that:

his name, liveth with his Ka.

3. The Spirit-Soul (Khu)

The khu is a higher spiritual element. It is a shining and luminous component. Khu-s are also heavenly beings living with the neteru (gods, goddesses). Each khu may then be equivalent to the guardian angel.

The Khu is mentioned in connection with the Ba and the Khaibit (soul and shadow), and with the Ba and the Ka (soul and double), but it is clear that it is something quite distinct from the Ka, Ba, and Khaibit; though in some respects it must have possessed characteristics similar to these immaterial entities of man.

4. Khai-bit

Khaibit is the shadow or shade—that which intercepts the light. This seems to have been an entity that served to focus or unite the lower Ka-s with all their carnal appetites and desires. The khai-bit seems to correspond with our notion of the ghost that appears mostly at cemeteries.

Baladi Egyptians believe that each person has a shadow—a separate entity—that follows him in life, dies, and goes to the grave with him.

It is of interest to note that the Egyptian word 'Khai' means companion/brother.

5. Ba—The Heart-Soul (Etheric Body)

While component #3 above is khu the *spirit soul*, the 5th component here represents the *heart soul*.

Later on, we will find *heart Ab* [Ba spelled in reverse] as the 7th component.

It must always be remembered that the term *heart* does not mean a physical human organ, but consciousness.

Therefore Ba as the heart-soul represents the totality of man's vital forces that include both physical and psychic capacities. As such, the Ba is depicted as a man-headed bird.

The Benu bird represents the totality of the concept of Ba in the universe.

In the cycle of creation that reflects the role of the dual Ra and Osiris/Aus-Ra, the Bennu bird is referred to as both *Ba of Ra* and Ba of Osiris/Aus-Ra—the all-encompassing BA.

In summary, the Ba represents:

– External manifestation

– Embodiment of power/vital force

The manifestation of power or power manifested cannot exist independently (of the body); and therefore the human Ba must maintain contact with body.

6. The Ka or Double (Astral Body)

Ka is the power that fixes and makes individual the animating spirit that is BA.

Ka is the complex of attractive or magnetic powers whose result is what today we would call personality: the pervading sense of "I" that inhabits the body but that is not the body. ("I" may be present even when the sense of body is lost entirely as in total paralysis or certain kinds of anesthesia.)

The Ka is complex.

1. There is the animal Ka concerned with the desires of the body;

2. the divine Ka that heeds the call of the spirit; and

3. the intermediate Ka, which provides the impetus to those on the path for gradually gaining control of the animal Ka and placing it in the service of the divine Ka.

At the root of the Ka concept lies the conviction that conscious, active life is not the function of the body, but rather flows from a higher power that activates the body and is thus the actual vehicle of life. The vital power is the Ka. There is no conscious life without it. It exists only by means of its effect.

When the body was born, there came into existence with it an abstract individuality or spiritual being which was wholly independent and distinct from the physical body, but its abode was the body, whose actions it was supposed to direct, guide, and keep watch over; and it lived in the body until the body died. No healthy child was ever born without this spiritual being, and when the Egyptians drew pictures of it, they always made it resemble the body to which it belonged. In other words, they regarded it as its "DOUBLE". Its name in Egyptian was Ka.

Ka, being double, is the double/image of its Ba.

7. The Heart (Ab)

The Ab is the heart, which corresponds to conscience. (Reverse Ba = heart-soul)

Horus is called the "dweller in hearts", the "lord of hearts", and the "slayer of the heart."

8. Sahu

Sahu is defined as a Spirit-body—the metaphysical [spiritual] body.

The Ancient Egyptians never expected the physical body to rise again – on the contrary, the texts state clearly that *the soul is in heaven, the body in the earth*". Egyptians believed that some kind of body rose from the dead and continued its existence in the Other World.

The spirit body was enabled to rise from the physical body through the rites and ceremonies that were performed over it.

On the day of burial by proper prayers and rituals, the physical body has the power of changing into a Sahu, a metaphysical (spiritual) body; awake.

Spiritual body = lasting and incorruptible

Ancient Egyptian texts read:

I flourish/sprout like the plants
My flesh flourisheth

The body that becomes a Sahu has the power of associating with the soul and of holding converse with it. It can ascend and dwell with neteru (gods, goddesses) in their **Sahus**.

Sahu, shown as mummy lying on a bier, indicates a spirit body that is lasting and incorruptible.

The word "sahu" seems to mean something like "free", "noble", or "chief"; and in this case it appears to be used as the name for a body which has, by means of the religious ceremonies that have been performed over it, obtained freedom from the material body and power whereby it has become incorruptible and ever-lasting.

Hence there arose the great importance of funeral ceremonies and offerings, which caused a spiritual body to spring from the physical body and the Ka to continue its existence after the death of the body to which it belonged.

Through powers of prayers and ritual, the body can change into Sahu, like the Two Sisters [Isis and Nephthys] awakening (Sahu) Osiris.

As the physical body formed the abiding-place of the Ka and the soul, so the spiritual body was believed to afford a dwelling-place for the soul; for it is distinctly said that "souls enter into their Sahu." And the spiritual body had power to journey everywhere in heaven and on earth.

9. Khat

Khat is defined as a physical/natural body—corruptible.

Khat – Meaning corruptible—is the reverse of Akh (luminous, incorruptible).

Khat is subject to decay, but could also refer to a mummified body.

The above shows the nine components in descending order from their divine origin. From earth, and moving upwards through the levels, is a process of shedding these different "sheaths" and moving through the various realms to the highest point of which the soul is capable before it descends again in rebirth.

Chapter 16 : Social & Political System

16.1 HARMONIC MATRILINEAL/MATRIARCHAL SOCIETY

Herodotus, in 500 BCE, stated: "Of all the nations of the world, Egyptians are the happiest, healthiest, and most religious". These are the three elements—happy, healthy, and religious—of the ideal society. The reason for such an ideal society is their total cosmic consciousness.

What we consider to be a "political" structure was, for them, a natural aspect of their social structure. In order to achieve perfect universal harmony, the social structure must mirror the same orderly hierarchy of the created universe. Human survival and success require that the same orderly structure be maintained.

As above so below is the only way to achieve order and harmony. As a result, the Ancient Egyptians (and Baladi) adopted the matrilineal/matriarchal system as the social manifestation of planetary laws.

As we have seen earlier, the Divine female principle is that Isis represents the sun and her husband Osiris represents the moon. The light of the moon (Osiris-male) is a reflection of the light of the sun (Isis-female). The Ancient Egyptian social/political system complies with the relationship between the sun (female) and the moon (male).

Isis' Egyptian name means *seat* (i.e., *authority*) and is the principle of legitimacy—the actual physical throne, as depicted in the Ancient Egyptian symbolism with Isis wearing a throne/seat upon her head.

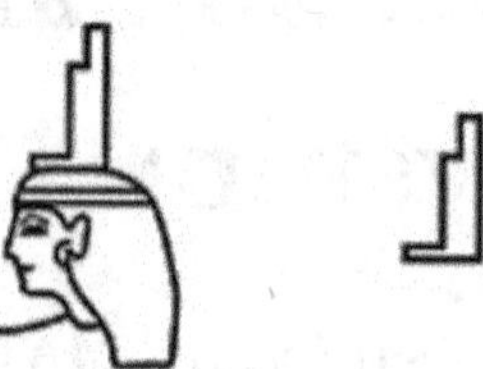

Ausar (Osiris) is written in hieroglyphs with the glyph of the throne and the eye, combining the concepts of legitimacy and divinity.

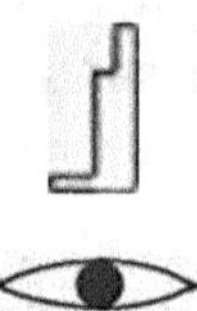

Throughout Egyptian history, it was the queen who transmitted the solar blood. The queen was the true sovereign, keeper of the royalty, and guardian of the lineage's purity. Egyptian kings claimed a right to the throne through marriage to the eldest Egyptian princess. By marriage, she transmitted the crown to her husband, but he only acted as her executive agent.

The pharaohs, as well as the leaders of smaller localities, adhered to this matriarchal system. If the pharaoh/leader had no daughters, then a dynasty ended and a new dynasty began, with a new revered maiden woman as a new seed for a new dynasty.

Since women were the legal heirs to the throne, they played an important part in the affairs of state, performing as a kind of power broker. The queens of Egypt wielded exceptional influence as advisers to the pharaohs.

Surviving records from the Middle Kingdom (2040–1783 BCE)

show that the nomes (provinces) of Egypt passed from one family to another through heiresses; thus, he who married the heiress would govern the province.

The matrilineal practices in Egypt also applied to the whole society, as evident from the funerary stelae of all kinds of people throughout the known recorded history of Egypt, where it is the usual custom to trace the descent of the deceased on the mother's side and not on that of the father. The person's mother is specified, but not the father; or if he is mentioned, it is only incidentally.

This tradition is still enduring secretly (because it is contrary to Islam) among the Baladi Egyptians.

[For more information about the matrilocal communities in Egypt, read *Ancient Egyptian Culture Revealed* by this same author.]

16.2 THE DUAL OVERSEEING/ADMINISTRATION SYSTEM

On every level of government (or, more correctly, public administration)—from the smallest matrilocal community and all the way to the whole country of Egypt —there was a dual governing system. In many ways, this system of dual governing continues in our present time. In the case of Britain, there is the British monarch as the head of state, who is the head of the Church of England and who inherits the throne according to specific precedence. However, the British monarch does not run the daily affairs, which are run by a prime minister who presides/oversees the work of the various ministries/departments. The prime minister is acting on behalf of the monarch, even though the prime minister (and his political party) are elected by the people. We even find similar dual systems of governing in countries with no monarchs, such as Germany and Israel, between a president and chancelor/prime minister.

Similarly—in conceptual format—at the head of the Ancient Egyptian society was the pharaoh, who represented the cosmic link between the natural (earthly) and supernatural (divine) powers. His role was not to rule, but to perform rituals to maintain the welfare of the society.

The pharaoh deputed his authority to the supreme/chief judge/ governor to run the daily affairs, one who was known since at least the Old Kingdom era (2575–2150 BCE) as the *Second after the King*. He was the chief of the whole administration. Each province (nome) was governed under the same dual system of spiritual and administrative leaders.

This dual system was tailored after the Ancient Egyptian cosmic allegorical prototypal system of government between Amen-Re (King of the Universe) and the governor (Thoth, the neter (god) of wisdom—the Wise Tongue/Sound/Voice). Thoth is thus the model executive and the official spokesperson.

The Ancient Egyptian governor was also known as the chief judge. The verb-stem of the Egyptian word for governor, (qadi) is qada, which means *to get done*; thus the term qadi, in the larger sense, means 'the executive'. The chief judge and governor presided over the head (executives/judges) of the various departments called the great/public houses such as agriculture, treasury, etc.

Likewise, on the regional and/or local levels, the office of governor was at all times of the highest importance, and to his charge were committed the management of the lands and all matters relating to the district's internal administration. He (and his supporting superintendents) regulated the survey of the lands, the opening of the canals, all agricultural and communal projects, commerce, and all other interests of the community/district/ province/country. All causes respecting landed property and other accidental disputes were referred to the executive judge and adjusted before his tribunal.

The "governor" was the Chief Executive Officer who executed the policies and laws as established by the legislative branch, the Council of Elders.

The smallest matrilocal community had a leader/king who governed with a council of elders. The council of elders, as representatives of their families, were equivalent to the legislative branch. They established policies and acted as final arbitrators (judges), if they needed to. The leader (and council) appointed/selected an administrator (governor, judge) to run the daily affairs. He had superintendents for various communal activities. He would arbitrate in cases that couldn't be resolved at lower levels.

[For more information about the Ancient Egyptian society such as the population's composition, nature, characteristics, etc., as well as the Grassroots Republic System, other political, administration, judiciary, economical, farming, manufacturing, transportation, trade, etc., read *Ancient Egyptian Culture Revealed* by same author.]

16.3 THE TENANTS' RIGHTS & OBLIGATIONS

The Ancient and Baladi Egyptian beliefs in Animism were also reflected in their traditional relationships between people and earth. The Egyptians believed/believe that land had no value apart from people; and, conversely, that people could not exist without land. They recognize and respect the supernatural residents of the land—any land. The spirits of a place (trees, rock outcroppings, rivers, snakes, and other animals and objects) were identified and placated by the original founders, who arrived and inhabited the land at an earlier time. The spirits of the land might vary with each place, or be so closely identified with a group's welfare that they were carried to a new place as part of the continuity of a group with its former home.

The rights of a group, defined by common genealogical descent, were linked to a particular place and the settlements within it (not through "ownership") because of their pact with the primordial spirits of the land/site. The spirits, both of family and place, demanded loyalty to communal virtues and to the authority of the elders in maintaining ancient beliefs and practices.

Newcomers (spiritual migrants) join the local spirit population in a new covenant between themselves and the local spirits. This covenant legitimized their arrival. In return for regular homage to these spirits, the founders could claim perpetual access to local resources. In so doing, they became the lineage in charge of the hereditary local priesthood and village headship, and were/are recognized as "tenants of the place" by later human arrivals.

The Ancient Egyptian transformational (funerary) texts maintain the same theme regarding the tenants' rights and obligations. As such, a new spirit must gain the acceptance and support of previous spirits in each of the realms of the "other world". [More details in chapter 21.]

This spirit of Animism makes people environmentalists, for they treat everything with care and respect. Such coexistence with nature in all its forms was a mandatory requirement of each person. Here are a few of the 42 Negative Confessions that emphasize that one must be a true environmentalist in order to succeed in reuniting with the Source:

> 7- *I have not plundered the neteru* (gods, goddesses).
> 16 – *I have not laid waste the ploughed land.*
> 22 – *Ihave not polluted myself.*
> 34 – *I have not fouled the water.*
> 36 – *I have never cursed the neteru* (gods, goddesses).

Such respect for the spirits of the land is indicative of a peaceful

(non-invasive) people who will not violate anybody or any land.
Egyptians, as such, are very peaceful people.

To the Ancient and Baladi Egyptians, stepping on a foreign land
in peace or in war was done with careful consideration to the
land and all its inhabitants, human and otherwise.

Chapter 17 : The Cosmic Link

17.1 THE ETERNAL POWER

Contrary to the Bible and Hollywood's distorted image of the pharaoh as a harsh tyrant living a luxurious, useless, and easy life, the pharaoh had no political power, lived in a mud-brick dwelling, and spent his time performing his duty to act as intermediary between the natural and supernatural worlds by conducting rites and sacrifices.

Pharaohs were not expected to be leaders of victorious armies, but were expected to secure a regular succession of rich harvests.

The pharaoh was the source of prosperity and well-being of the state, to his people. He was their servant; not their tyrant. He laid the seeds at the beginning of the season and collected the "fruit" at harvest time. He spent his time serving the interests of his people by performing necessary rituals throughout the whole country. The pharaohs were identified with the crops and were addressed as: *Our Crop* and *Our Harvest.*

Based on his extensive training with the powers of the supernatural, the Pharaoh's body was believed to be charged with a divine dynamism that communicated itself to everything he touched. Diodorus reported that the Pharaoh typically led a restricted life. Not even the most intimate of his courtiers might see him eat or drink. When the King ate, he did so in private. The food was offered to him with the same ritual as was used by priests in offering sacrifice to the neteru (gods, goddesses).

The right to rule was considered to be a continuous chain of legitimacy which was based on matriarchal principles where the line of royal descent in Egypt was through the eldest daughter. Whoever she married became the pharaoh. If the pharaoh did not beget a daughter, a new "dynasty" was formed. There was no "royal blood" in Ancient Egypt.

The eternal power of the leader/King never dies. The power is merely transferred from one human body to another human body (medium). Accordingly, all the Pharaohs identified themselves with Horus as a *living* King and with the soul of Osiris as a *dead* King.

This is eloquently illustrated in several places in Ancient Egyptian tombs and temples, as shown below, whereby Horus is being born out of Osiris after his death.

Even the British of today follow, unconsciously, the same belief that the eternal power transfers from one human body to another, when they say:

"The king is dead. Long live the king."

as if to say:

"Osiris is dead. Long live Horus."

17.2 THE MASTER SERVANT

The Ancient Egyptian King, with the help of the priests associated with him and via the ancestral spirits, established a proper relationship between the people and the supernatural forces. The leader was regarded as having a personal influence over the works of nature, to whom divine honors were paid and to whom divine powers were attributed.

The Ancient Egyptian Pharaoh was an earthly image of the sum of divine energies of the universe (neteru). As such, he continually performed the necessary rituals for proper relationship and communication with the neteru (the powers of the universe) in order to maintain the welfare of the state and to insure the fertility of the earth, that it may bring forth sustenance.

Each year, the King hoed the first plot of farming land and sowed the first seeds. If the Pharaoh did not perform the daily liturgy to the neteru (gods, goddesses), the crops would perish. He spent his time performing his duties to his people by performing the necessary rituals, from one temple to another, throughout the whole country.

Despite the repeated charges of vanity against the Pharaohs, it is worth remembering that their abodes while on earth were never made of stone, but of mud brick, the same material used by the humblest peasants. These humble mortal monarchs believed that the impermanent body, formed of clay by Khnum, the ram-headed neter, called for an equally impermanent abode on this earth. The earthly houses of the Kings have long since returned to the earth from which they were raised.

17.3 KEEPING THE FLAME ALIVE [THE HEB-SED FESTIVAL]

The fertility of the soil, the abundant harvests, the health of people and cattle, the normal flow of events, and all phenomena of life were/are intimately linked to the potential of the ruler's vital force. It is therefore that the Egyptian king was not supposed (or even able) to reign unless he was in good health and spirits.

Accordingly, he was obliged to rejuvenate his vital force by regularly attending physical and metaphysical practices which are known as the Heb-Sed rituals.

The purpose of the Ancient Egyptian annual Heb-Sed festival (which was regularly held towards the end of December) was to renew the pharaoh's power in a series of rituals including ritual sacrifice. The renewal rituals were aimed at bringing a new life force to the king; i.e. a (figurative) death and a (figurative) rebirth of the reigning king. One of the Heb-Sed rituals was to induce a near-death experience so that the king could travel to the higher realms to rejuvenate his cosmic powers. When he returned, he would be a "new" king. This gives more meaning to the phrase:

The King is dead—Long Live the King.

17.4 THE PEOPLE RULE

The Pharaoh's conduct and mode of life were regulated by prescribed rules, since his main function was to ensure the prosperity and well-being of his subjects. Laws were laid down in the sacred books for the order and nature of his occupations.

He was forbidden to commit excesses. Even the kind and quality of his foods were prescribed with precision. Even if the king had the means of defying prescribed rules, the voice of the people could punish him at his death by the disgrace of excluding his body from burial in his own tomb.

When the body of the deceased king was placed in state near the entrance of his tomb, the assembled people were asked if anyone objected to the king's entombment because he did not perform his duties. If the public showed their dissent by loud murmurs, he was deprived of the honor of the customary public funeral and burial in his tomb.

The body of an unaccomplished Egyptian pharaoh, though

excluded from the burial at the necropolis, was not refused his right to be buried somewhere else. A case in point is the communal gravesite that was found in 1876 in the immediate vicinity of the Hatshepsut Commemorative (wrongly known as "Mortuary") Temple on the West Bank of the River Nile at Luxor (Thebes). Those whose performances were unsatisfactory to the common populace were buried at this location. Such rejected pharaohs included the mummies of well-recognized and influential names such as Amenhotep I, Tuthomosis II and III, Seti I, and Ramses I and III.

As will be shown later in this book, Egyptian texts clearly state that the Egyptian king can only have his place in Heaven if he:

> *__hath not been spoken against on earth before men__, he hath not been accused of sin in heaven before the neteru* (gods, goddesses)."

17.5 THE VICTORIOUS KING

In Ancient Egyptian temples, tombs, and texts, human vices are depicted as foreigners (the sick body is sick because it is/was invaded by foreign germs). Foreigners are depicted as subdued—arms tightened/tied behind their backs—to portray inner self-control.

The most vivid example of self control is the common depiction of the Pharaoh (The Perfected Man) on the outer walls of Ancient Egyptian temples, subduing/controlling foreign enemies (the enemies [impurities] within). It symbolizes the forces of order controlling chaos and the light triumphing over darkness.

The same "war" scene is repeated at temples throughout the country, which signifies its symbolism and is not necessarily a representation of actual historical events.

The "war" scenes symbolize the never-ending battle between Good and Evil. In many cases there is no historical basis for such war scenes, even though a precise date is given. Such is the case for the war scenes on the Temple Pylon at Medinat Habu.

Western academicians are incapable of understanding metaphysical realities, and hence "make" historical events out of metaphysical concepts. The famed "Battle of Kadesh" is really the personal drama of the individual royal man (the king in each of us) single-handedly subduing the inner forces of chaos and darkness. Kadesh means *holy/sacred*.

Therefore, the Battle of Kadesh signifies the inner struggle—a holy war within each individual.

Chapter 18 : The Physical/ Metaphysical Society

18.1 SEEKING HEAVENLY HIGHER-UPS

The Ancient and Baladi Egyptians made/make no distinction between a metaphysical state of being and one with a material body. Such a distinction is a mental illusion, as accepted now in scientific circles since Einstein's relativity theory that *matter is a form of energy.*

Just as our lives do not stop at death, so our bodies are not limited by their outer physical forms. We exist on a number of different levels at once, from the most physical to the most spiritual. Indeed, in one sense, there is no difference between physical and spiritual; only the gradations that lie between the two ends of the spectrum.

The universal energy matrix, according to the Egyptian traditions, consists of the unity of nine (7 heavens and 2 lands) interpenetrating and interactive realms. As such, Ancient and Baladi Egyptians maintained/maintain communications between their earthly realm and the spirits/energies of the 'other world'.

The Egyptians made two broad distinctions in the hierarchical metaphysical structure of the seven heavens:

A. At the highest end of this celestial order, there exists three levels in a sort of heavenly court or council that are not involved with human activities on earth. Such realms are the equivalents of the Archangels and the Orders of Angels which we find in other systems of religion.

B. The Egyptians distinguished four lower groups that occupy the celestial hierarchy positions that consist of those who lived on earth for one time or another, and after their earthly departure, continue to be involved with human activities on earth. Such realms are identical with those of some Oriental Christian systems, the prophets, apostles, martyrs, and many great saints.

In all periods of Egyptian history, a class of beings was known; some of whom are male and some female. These had many forms and shapes and could appear on earth as men, women, animals, birds, reptiles, trees, plants, etc. They were stronger and more intelligent than men, but they had passions like men. They were credited with possessing some divine powers or characteristics, and yet they could suffer sickness and die.

Egyptians speak of their deceased as living, which shows how definite a belief it is that the souls of the deceased return to their tombs/shrines on the specified days of their weekly and annual visitations.

18.2 THE HEAVENLY HELPERS

We will highlight here the most common heavenly helpers, as being:

i – Family and close relatives

The most common communications were/are between earthly beings and their ancestor spirits. These spirits serve the needs of individual family members.

ii – Community Patrons—[Ancestral local/regional patrons]

The character of such departed souls as community patrons

["local god"] covers a broad range, fulfilling the expectation of their descendants in the community at large. They behave like superior human beings with the same passions and the same needs; but also with transcendental power. The city is the "House" of the 'patron'. They have shrines, holy objects, and statues. They may appear in the form of stones, trees, animals or human beings.

It is conceivable that the patron of a particularly great and mighty town should be believed to exercise a sort of patronage, either politically or agriculturally, over an extended area, and the power they had attained determined their expanding influence over a larger area, resulting in them becoming a great patron with extensive territory.

Certain shrines show them to be purely local patrons; many being originally called after towns such as "him of Ombos", "him of Edfu", "her of Bast" – they are really merely the genii of the towns. Many show themselves to their followers in the form of some object in which they dwelt. The Egyptians believed that each place was inhabited by a great number of spirits, and that the lesser ones were subject to the chief spirit.

The local/village patron is visited weekly every Thursday or Friday. In addition, they have their seasonal and annual festivals.

iii – Folk Saints

Walis (folk saints) are the people who succeeded in traveling the spiritual Path and who, as a result, have attained union with the Divine. Such unification enables them to perform supernatural acts, influence and predict future events, etc. As a result, they become the intermediaries between the earthly living beings and the supernatural, heavenly realms.

After their earthly death, their spiritual force/blessing is thought to increase and to reside in the persons and particularly the places associated with and chosen by them. A folk saint chooses and conveys the places for his shrines to his family and friends during dreams (and possibly waking consciousness, also). As a result, a shrine (or more—usually more than two) is set apart for him/her. Such shrines, in most cases, are not their tombs. These shrines dot the Egyptian landscape since its earliest known history.

Ancient and Baladi Egyptians stayed/stay in touch with the Walis. People regularly visit the Walis at their shrines, from surrounding communities. It is a social obligation to visit them; especially on his/her mouled (annual celebration).

In addition to visitations, people may also ask these Walis for personal favors. Vows are made by individuals that if the Wali resolves a personal concern, the vower will donate certain items to charity.

Unlike the Christian saints, Walis are chosen by ordinary people based on performance. Once the people can see that this person does indeed have the ability to influence supernatural forces in order to assist those on earth and, as a result, fulfills their wishes; then s/he is recognized as a Wali.

These folk saints are mistakenly called "minor gods' by Western writers.

[For more information about folk-saints, festivals, etc., read *Egyptian Mystics: Seekers of the Way* by Moustafa Gadalla.]

18.3 ORDERLY RELEASE OF METAPHYSICAL BODIES [FUNERARY RITES]

The existence of funeral rites in any society reflects the belief that something essential survives man's physical death, and that the mode of burial in some way influences existence in that spiritual region.

Hence arose the great importance of funeral ceremonies and offerings, which caused a spiritual body to spring from the physical body and the 'Ka' to continue its existence after the death of the body to which it belonged.

Correct rituals are pre-requisites to the process of leaving this realm in an orderly manner to go to another one. Also, correct rituals ensure the return of the deceased during festivals, etc.

The Egyptians believed in a future life. Now we have to try to find out, from their religious literature,

> (1) what portion of a man's entity it was which lived after the death of his body;
> (2) what form it lived in; and
> (3) where it lived

When the body died, there could be raised from it (by means of words holy or magical and ceremonies performed by the priests) a Spirit-body called Sahu (#8) which entered heaven and lived with the blessed for all eternity.

The Ka (#6), Ba (#5), and Shadow Khabet (#4) dwelt in the tomb with the body or wandered about outside it and away from it, when they desired to do so. Their existence was finite, and appears to have terminated whenever funerary offerings failed to be made to them.

For more information about the roles and interactions between these metaphysical components, refer to The Nine Components of Man in Chapter 15.

18.4 THE MEDIATING TREES—SACRED GROVE

Trees, as part of the animated universe, act as a convenient medium between the earthly and departed souls. The Egyptian term for sacred grove is *Ginne-na/Guineana*, meaning *the place of ancestor spirits*.

Just as the Christmas tree is important in Christmas traditions, where it mediates between Saint Nick and his followers, so we find likewise in the Egyptian traditions, where every folk-saint (Wali) shrine must be next to a tree.

Offerings of food and drinks are left beneath the tree of the saint.

The same trees are the places for contemplation.

All types of rituals were conducted next to the Holy Tree.

The tree mediates the resurrection, returning back to life.

In the Isis/Osiris allegory, Osiris was enshrined in a living tree.

If a gin (ancestor) tree (a tree with a spirit living in it) is nearby, people often write notes and attach them to the branches of the tree.

Wise men and women consult departed spirits constantly, and periodically spend several days with them at the spirited grove.

[More about trees and landscape architecture in our book, *The Ancient Egyptian Metaphysical Architecture*, by Moustafa Gadalla.]

18.5 THE WESTERN WALL THRESHOLD

On the western side of ALL Egyptian temples and tombs there is always a crack in the wall, or what is commonly described as a *false door*. The door was a monolithic limestone "false" door, with torus molding and a cavetto cornice.

The false door was for the use of the departed, and it was believed that the ghost entered or left it at will. It acted as the interface between the divine and human spheres.

The term 'false door' is itself something of a misnomer as, from the Egyptian perspective, these features were fully functional portals by which the spirit of the deceased might leave or enter the inner tomb to receive the offerings presented to them.

The west is the point of entry of the departed spirit. It is the threshold between the physical earthly realm and the meta-physical realm. As such, the western wall defines the interface between the public and the departed. The smallest tomb in present-day Egypt would have a false door or a hole/crack in the western wall where the living talk to the deceased.

[For design details of burial and non burial visitation sites, read *The Ancient Egyptian Metaphysical Architecture* by Moustafa Gadalla.]

18.6 THE COSMIC SHRINES (TEMPLES)

The Egyptian temples were not built for public worship, but as shrines for the neteru (gods, goddesses) who represent the different powers of the One God. The Egyptian temple is the link – the proportional mean – between the Macro-cosmos (world) and Micro-cosmos (man). It was a stage upon which meetings were enacted between the neter/netert (god/goddess) and the King, as a representative of the people.

The Egyptian temple was a machine for maintaining and developing divine energy. It was the place in which the cosmic energy, neter/etert (god/goddess), came to dwell and radiate its energy to the land and people.

Only after the neteru (gods, goddesses) had examined the temple destined for them did they come and dwell there, as clearly stated in this Ancient Egyptian text:

> *When the great winged scarab rises from the primordial ocean and sails through the heavens in the guise of Horus ...he stops in the heaven before this temple and his heart is filled with joy*

as he looks at it. Then he becomes one with his image, in his favorite place.'

The walls of the Egyptian temple were covered with animated images—including hieroglyphs—to facilitate the communication between the Above and the Below.

Understanding this function helps us to regard Egyptian art as something vital and alive. Therefore, we must forego viewing the temple as an interplay of forms against a vague historical and archaeological presentation. Instead, we must try to see it as the relationship between form and function.

The harmonious power of the temple plans, the images engraved on the walls, and the forms of worship all led to the same goal; a goal that was both spiritual (as it involved setting superhuman forces in motion) and practical (in that the final awaited result was the maintenance of the country's prosperity).

The temple's rituals were based upon and coordinated with the movements of the heavens which were, in turn, manifestations of divine cosmic law.

The temple's rituals included, among other things, presenting material offerings: bread, beer, rolls of linen, meat, fowl, and other goods.

The natures of material objects were transmuted into spirit entities when they were laid upon consecrated altars. The character of the Egyptian offering is shown by the common word for offering, *hetep*, which means a *gift of peace*, or *propitiation*. The stone or wooden tablet upon which the offerings were laid is also called *hetep*. The altar was believed to possess the power of transmuting the offerings that were laid upon it, turning them into spiritual entities of such a nature that they became suitable "food" for the neteru/spirits. In other words, the neteru (gods, goddesses) consume only the spirits (or "doubles") of the bread, beer, vegetables, meat, oil, etc. [More about offerings later in this chapter.]

[More information about the design and construction of the temples is in *The Ancient Egyptian Metaphysical Architecture* by same author.]

18.7 THE CYCLICAL RENEWAL FESTIVALS

The main theme of the Ancient Egyptian texts is the cyclical nature of the universe and the constant need for the renewal of such cycles through well-designated festivals.

The Egyptians viewed/view these festivals as part of human existence, which constitutes the rhythm of the life of the community and of the individual. This rhythm results from the order of cosmic life.

The renewal and rejuvenation of the life of the cosmos, of the community, and of the individual are affected by rites. These rites had/have the power to bring about the rejuvenation and rebirth of divine life. Failure to hold the festivals at the appropriate dates and times might very well produce individual or collective sentiments of culpability. As such, the Egyptian festivals came to have the function of enactments of cosmological (religious) renewals.

Most of the Egyptians not only expect a blessing to follow their participation, but they also dread that some misfortune will befall them if they neglect this act.

The aim of the Egyptian festivals was (and continues to be) the rejuvenation and renewal of the cosmic energies. During the numerous Ancient Egyptian religious festivals, the participants fall back on the archetypal truth of their cosmic consciousness (As above so below, and as below so above). Every holy festival actualizes the archetypal holy cycle. These holy cycles have become part of the calendar. More accurately, the calendar served to indicate when the cosmological powers (neteru/gods) were manifested, and their renewal cycles. All early Greek and Roman writers affirmed these Ancient Egyptian cosmic correlations, such as Plutarch, in his *Moralia Vol. V* (377,65):

> *... They [the Egyptians] associate theological concepts*
> *with the seasonal changes in the surrounding atmosphere,*
> *or with the growth of the crops and seed-times and plowing.*

All the elements and rules governing the Ancient Egyptian festivals are exactly applicable to present-day festivals with organized and detailed schemes. Baladi Egyptians continue to consider the festivals and their rituals as the climax of their religious practices, which are very critical to the order and harmony of the cosmos and, by extension, the well-being of one and all.

All present-day festivals (except for Mohammed's and those of his immediate family) are a continuation of Ancient Egyptian festivals, camouflaged under Islamic names.

The official annual number of festivals (mouleds) in present-day Egypt, even though they are contrary to Islam, is estimated at more than 3,000. There is not a single day in Egypt without a mouled somewhere, and the participation is very profound. The major Autumn mouled of elBadawi is attended by more than two million people and each of the other two mouleds are attended, respectively, by more than one million visitors.

All this is indicative of the Baladi Egyptians' adherence by the millions to their ancient traditions.

[For more information read *Egyptian Mystics: Seekers of The Way* by same author.]

18.8 THE PHYSICAL/METAPHYSICAL OFFERINGS

The energy matrix of the physical body will disintegrate—weaken and ultimately die—if it is not provided with food and drink.

Likewise, a departed spirit (energy matrix) requires sustenance; otherwise it will disintegrate, decompose, or convert into other forms of energies. In simple terms, departed souls are always hungry and thirsty, and so must be supplied with food and drink.

As stated earlier, the spirits/energies of the higher realms only consume the spirit of the offerings.

The Ancient and Baladi Egyptians made offerings to the spirits of their ancestors with the intention of keeping their help and protection by maintaining their existence. Their existence was finite, and appears to have terminated whenever funerary offerings failed to be made to them on a regular basis. Neglect would cause them to lose the force that helped those still living on earth.

The idea of offering should not be strange to the Western mind, since they are familiar with presenting bread and wine in church services [or placing flowers at sites to honor deceased].

It is important to know the Egyptian word for offering, which is *Qurban*, derived from the stem verb QaRaB, meaning: *to be near to*. The meaning now becomes clear: the intent is to stay near/ close to the departed souls.

Inscriptions in various Egyptian temples and tomb chapels, as well as in a number of letters, testify to the importance of such rituals. One of these letters, for example, speaks of:

> *"my daughter who makes offerings to the spirit in return* (gods, goddesses) *for watching over the earthly survivors."*

Diodorus, in *Book I*, 16, affirms the role of Thoth as it relates to the significance of offerings and the ordinances required to maintain them:

*It was by Thoth, according to the Egyptians, that . . .
and that ordinances regarding the honors and offerings
due to the neteru (gods, goddesses)were duly established. . .*

[More about the various types of individual and group offerings is found in the book *Egyptian Mystics: Seekers of The Way* by same author.]

Chapter 19 : Astronomical Consciousness

19.1 COSMIC CONSCIOUSNESS AND ASTRONOMY

Egypt, recognizing the influence of the heavens on earth, observed the skies with the utmost attention. The data of astronomy was studied for its meaning: that is to say, the study of correspondences between events in the heavens and events on earth. Astronomy and astrology were, for them, two sides of the same coin.

Ancient Egyptian records of all subject matters show a complete coordination and correspondence between Egyptians' activities on earth and the various cycles of the universe (as some applications are described throughout this book).

The Egyptians were very much aware of their dependence on the cycles of earth and sky. Therefore, temple priests were assigned the task of observing the movements of these heavenly bodies. They were also responsible for noting other celestial events and interpreting them.

Numerous monuments can be found throughout Ancient Egyptian sites, attesting to their full awareness and knowledge of cosmology and astronomy.

Clement Alexandrinus (200 CE) reported about the advanced knowledge of astronomy in Ancient Egypt. He referred to five interrelated volumes in Ancient Egypt on astronomy—one containing a list of the fixed stars, another on the phenomena of the sun and moon, two others on the rising of the stars, and another containing a cosmography and geography, the course of the sun, moon, and the five planets. These references indicate a complete understanding of astronomy unmatched even in our present times.

While Western academia attributes the knowledge of astronomy to the Greeks, the Greeks themselves attributed their astronomical knowledge to the Egyptian priests.

The Great Strabo [64 BCE–25 CE] admitted, in c. 20 BCE (about 100 years after Hipparchus) that:

> *The Egyptian priests are supreme in the science of the sky...[the Egyptians]...impart some of their precepts; although they conceal the greater part. [The Egyptians] revealed to the Greeks the secrets of the full year, whom the latter ignored as with many other things".*

(More about the most accurate Egyptian calendaral year later in this chapter.)

Astronomers studying Egypt have long argued that Egyptian astronomy was highly advanced; that the precession of the equinoxes was known to them, as was the heliocentric system and many other phenomena supposedly only recently discovered.

19.2 KEPLER AND EGYPTIAN ASTRONOMY

A few decades ago, those who suggested that astronomy had reached an advanced state long before the invention of the telescope were generally ridiculed or ignored. "Modern" astronomy is attributed to the works of Johannes Kepler [1571–1630 CE], and he is credited with having "discovered" the three planetary laws without the "benefit of a telescope".

Law 1. The orbit of a planet/comet about the sun is an ellipse with the sun's center of mass at one focus.

Law 2. A line joining a planet/comet and the sun sweeps out equal areas in equal intervals of time.

Law 3. The squares of the periods of the planets are proportional to the cubes of their semi-major axes.

Planetary laws that show the relationships between planets, distances, variations in speed, orbit configurations, etc. can never be determined without regular observations, measurements, recording, and analysis; yet none of these western academicians tell us how Kepler arrived (out of thin air) at these planetary laws. In truth, Kepler himself boasted in print, at the end of *Book V* of his series *Harmony of the World*, that he rediscovered the lost laws of Egypt, as stated below:

> *"Now, eighteen months after the first light, three months after the true day, but a very few days after the pure Sun of that most wonderful study began to shine, nothing restrains me; it is my pleasure to yield to the inspired frenzy, it is my pleasure to taunt mortal men with the candid acknowledgment that <u>I am stealing the golden vessels of the Egyptians</u> to build a tabernacle to my God from them, far, far away from the boundaries of Egypt".*

The jubilant Kepler did not state that he himself discovered anything. Rather, it was all Ancient Egyptian.

19.3 ASTRONOMICAL OBSERVATIONS AND RECORDINGS

Numerous monuments can be found throughout Ancient Egyptian sites, attesting to their full awareness and knowledge of cosmology and astronomy. A systematic kind of astronomical observation began in Ancient Egypt at a very early time. The

Ancient Egyptians compiled information, making charts of the constellations based on observations and recordings.

A systematic kind of astronomical observation began in very early times. The most ancient astronomical texts presently known are found on the lids of wooden coffins dating from the 9th Dynasty (c. 2150 BCE).

These texts are called *diagonal calendars* or *diagonal star clocks*, which signify the objectives and contents of these texts: to observe and document the relationship between the stars' movement and time.

The word 'diagonal' signifies measurement of angles; i.e., the arc distance of movement during a specific time period.

The angular measurements are in conjunction of the Egyptians division of the sky into 36 angular segments. Each has a 10-degrees central angle, for a total of 360 degrees.

These texts give the names of the decans (stars which rose at ten-day intervals at the same time as the sun), of which there were 36.

More elaborate star charts were found in the New Kingdom (1550–1070 BCE) on the ceiling of the tomb of Senenmut, Queen Hatshepsut's architect, and on the ceiling at the temple of Abydos. In the tombs of Set I and Ramses IV, VII, and IX, inscriptions that relate to the first and the 16th day of each month give the position occupied by a star at each of the 12 hours of the night in relation to a seated figure (over the left ear, over the right ear, etc.).

19.4 EGYPTIAN REAL TIMEKEEPING

The Ancient Egyptian knowledge of timekeeping is reflected in their division of the day into 12 hours of day and 12 hours of night. The length of the hour was not fixed, but varied with the seasons. Long days in the summer meant longer hours of the day and the opposite in the winter months. March 21 and September 23, when the sun crosses the equator and day and night are everywhere of equal length, are known as 'equinoxes' (equal nights). The variable length of the hour signifies their understanding of the equinox as well as their full understanding of accurate time measurement, as explained below.

Because the earth revolves around the sun in the plane of its orbit once each year, the reference line to the sun is changing constantly, and the length of one solar day is not the true time of one rotation of the earth. It is therefore that our "modern" astronomy recognizes that the true time of one rotation of the earth, which is known as the sidereal day, is based on one rotation with respect to the vernal equinox, when the length of day and night are exactly the same.

The Ancient Egyptians knew the secrets of time because they observed and studied the apparent motion of the stars, the moon, and the sun. Because all celestial bodies are in constant apparent motion with respect to the observer, it is extremely important to know the precise time of an observation of a celestial body—which the Ancient Egyptians mastered a long time ago.

The motion of each celestial body was measured in angular change as a combination of declination and right ascension; these being the given coordinates of the stars on a sky map.

The observations were recorded and plotted on a grid by superimposing—under the center of the sky—a human figure sitting upright, with the top of his head placed below the zenith. The grid was typically 8 horizontal segments and 12 vertical segments, representing the 12 hours of the night. The stars which were approaching the zenith were referenced over a portion of this figure, and their position was indicated in the lists of stars: over the left ear, over the right ear, etc.

The Ancient Egyptian astronomical texts give the position of the stars during the 12 hours of the night at intervals of 15 days, and from this information, the change in location of a particular point in the sky can be measured. These frequent, regular measurements and recordings led them to correlate the rate of speed of the heavenly bodies and, as such, the Ancient Egyptians were able to record major and minor irregularities in the perceived motion of these celestial bodies.

Maps of the heavens and star tables were made in Egypt from a very early date; the stars being grouped together to form constellations like those portrayed on the ceilings of the tomb. Astronomical references to the important constellation of the Bull Leg (Great Bear) to Sirius, to Orion, and to other star groups are found in the Pyramid Texts of the 5th and 6th dynasties.

Lists of the decans or ten day stars (or star groups) associated with hour star tables were already in use on the 11th and 12th dynasties' coffins from Assyut.

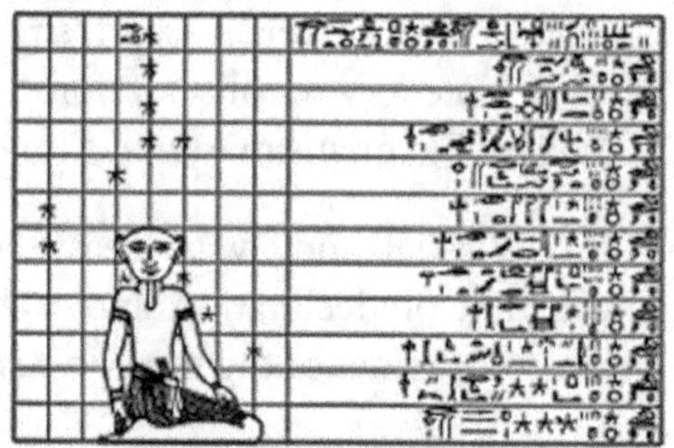

**List of stars on the 16th of Babeh (Paophi)—27 October—from Ramses
IX's tomb in Ta-Apet (Thebes).**

In the case of Ramses IX's (1131-1112 BCE) tomb, the ceiling shows the positions of the various stars over 12 consecutive 15-day periods. From these star charts, the Ancient Egyptians determined the positions and changes of location and/or time of stars. As such, the Ancient Egyptians were aware of the fact that the stars shifted slowly and that this was easily measurable at meridian transit; and thus the Ancient Egyptians knew and worked out the rate of precessional change.

The Ancient Egyptians made reference to the stars that define the perimeter of the various constellations, such as:

> leg of the giant
> claw of the goose
> head of the goose
> hinder-part of the goose
> star of thousands
> star S'ar
> finger-point of the constellation S'ah. (Orion)
> the stars of S'ah. (Orion)
> star that follows Sirius
> finger-point of twin-stars
> stars of the water
> point of finger of the S'ah.
> head of the lion
> tail of the lion

19.5 THE ZODIAC CYCLE

The star chart of the north pole of the sky from the tomb of Seti I [1333–1304 BCE] [shown above] reinforces the Ancient Egyptian meaning of the word zodiac as a circle of animals.

The main reason for our awareness on earth of the zodiac is the earth's wobble in its orbit movements around the sun The earth rotates from west to east on its polar axis and revolves about the sun in an elliptical orbit with the sun at one focus of the ellipse. It completes one revolution in a period of 365.2564 days. The inclination of the earth (23½ degrees perpendicular to the orbital plane), combined with its revolution around the sun, causes the lengths of day and night to change and also causes the different seasons [shown below].

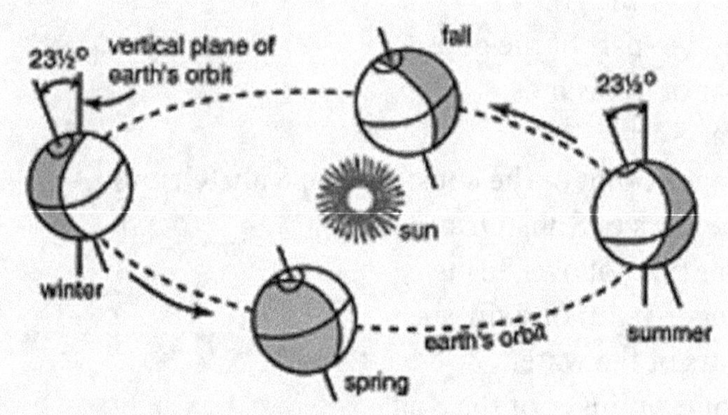

If the sky is regarded as a constellated backdrop, then because of the wobble of the earth upon its axis, the vernal equinox each year rises against a gradually shifting background of constellations. The effect is not real, but apparent, and only involves the stars. The stars do not actually move, but appear to move because of the earth's precessional wobble. Astronomers call this the *precession of the equinoxes*.

The continuous shifting of the stars' position acts as a sort of star-clock for our planet. For the Ancient Egyptians, by knowing the exact rate of precessional change and the coordinate of a star, they were able to determine its altitude at the meridian for any given time, or its rising point on the eastern horizon.

The precession of the equinoxes through the constellations gives names to the twelve zodiac ages. It takes roughly 2,160 years for the equinox to precess through a zodiac sign. Thus, it takes some

25,920 years for the spring equinox to traverse the full circuit of the constellations of the twelve zodiac signs. This complete cycle is called the Great/Full Year.

The signs of the zodiac are found in numerous locations throughout the history of Ancient Egypt. Here, the zodiac is represented in two locations at the Hathor Temple at Dendera. It is clearly Ancient Egyptian, with its figures, symbols, etc. The same exact symbolism of depicted zodiac ages, deities, figures, etc. were found in numerous Ancient Egyptian temples and tombs throughout the country long before the Greco-Roman era.

The circular zodiac [shown above] is depicted on the ceiling of the upper level of the temple, where the signs are arranged in a spiral form.

Pathetically, Western academia attempts to credit a *European* with this major achievement. Yet, in this case, Hipparchus (who never claimed himself as the source) **could never have single-handedly done something that requires astronomical observations, measurements, and recordings, for centuries and millennia.**

While Western academia attributes the knowledge of astronomy to the Greeks, the Greeks themselves attributed their astronomical knowledge to the Egyptian priests. The Great Strabo [64 BCE–25 CE] admitted in c. 20 BCE (about 100 years after Hipparchus) that:

> *"The Egyptian priests are supreme in the science of the sky...[the Egyptians]...impart some of their precepts; although they conceal the greater part. [The Egyptians] revealed to the Greeks the secrets of the full year, whom the latter ignored as with many other things..."*

19.6 IN RHYTHM WITH THE ZODIAC AGES

There is overwhelming and exhaustive evidence showing how Egypt responded to the different zodiac ages. There was a shift of symbolism from Leo (the lion) and Gemini (the twins) to Taurus (the bull) and Aries (the ram). These shifts coincided with the dates of the astronomical precession. Egyptians applied different means and modes of expression for each zodiac age, which were based upon the inherent specific nature of each age.

The last zodiac age in the Ancient Egyptian history was the Age of Aries (the Ram) [2307–148 BCE].

When the Age of Aries (the Ram) arrived, the Egyptian records revealed this new Age. Ram-headed figures dominated the Egyptian buildings. Ram-headed sphinxes were aligned at the entrance of the Karnak Temple [see illustration above].

19.7 THE SOTHIC CYCLE—THE LEADING STAR

During the very remote periods of Ancient Egyptian history, Isis was associated with the star Sirius, the brightest star in heaven, which was called, like her, *the Great Provider*. Egypt's ingenious and very accurate calendar was based on the observation and the study of Sirius' movements in the sky. This fact is clearly acknowledged in the Webster's dictionary, which defines the *Sothic year* as:

- of having to do with Sirius, the Dog Star

- Designating or of an Ancient Egyptian cycle or period of time based on fixed year.

The Egyptians' advanced knowledge in astronomy, as reflected in their calendar, was acknowledged by the great Strabo (64 BCE–25 CE), who wrote:

> *They (the Egyptian priests) revealed to the Greeks the secrets of the full year, whom the latter ignored as with many other things...*

The writing shown below is a memorandum from the Overseer of the temple to the Lectorpriest at Nubkaura Temple at el-Lahun (during the time of Senwosret II, 1897–1878 BCE), notifying him that Sirius would rise on the 16th day of the 4th month, so as to take note of its exact location and time and to enter it into the temple records.

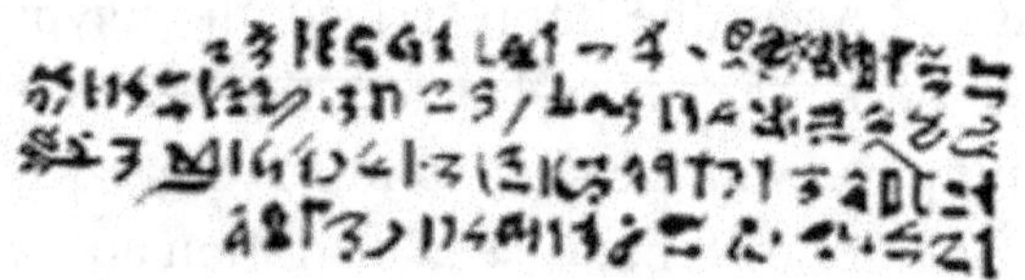

The Ancient Egyptians knew that the year was slightly over 365¼ days. The earth takes 365.25636 days to complete one revolution around the sun.

It should be noted that the chronology of 3,000 years of Ancient Egyptian history by modern Egyptologists was made possible only because of the accuracy of the Ancient Egyptian Sothic calendar that followed the heliacal rising of Sirius, the Dog Star, of its annual duration of 365.25636 days.

The practical Ancient Egyptians used a calendar consisting of 12 months; each equal to 30 days. The adjustments needed to make a complete year – i.e., the difference between 365.25636 days and the 360 (30 x 12) days – were made as follows:

1. The difference of 5.25 days comes at the end of the Egyptian year by adding 5 days every year and an additional day every 4 years. The Ancient Egyptian Year currently begins (in 2016) on 11 September. The 5/6 extra days begin on 6 September.

2. The difference of 0.00636 day (365.25636 – 365¼ days) for each year requires adding another day every (1/ 0.00636) 157¼ years, which the Egyptians continued to do until our present times. This is accomplished by adding an extra day every 157, 314, 471 and 629 year cycles. The above adjustments by the Egyptians can clearly be seen in the last 2,000 years when comparing the Ancient Egyptian calendar with the "Latin" calendar [as explained below].

The Greeks, Romans, and other ancient sources affirmed that the Egyptians regarded Sirius as the great central fire about which our solar system orbits. Sirius' movements are intimately associated with another companion star. Sirius and its companion are revolving around their common center of gravity (or, in other words, are revolving about each other). Sirius' diameter is less than twice the diameter of our sun. Its companion, however, has a diameter only about three times the diameter of Earth; yet it weighs about 250,000 times as much as the Earth. Its material is packed together so tightly that it is about 5,000 times as dense as lead. Such a compression of matter means that Sirius' companion's atoms do not exist in their normal states, but are squeezed so closely together that many atomic nuclei are crowded into a space previously occupied by a single normal atom; i.e., the electrons of these atoms are squeezed out of their orbits and move about freely (a degenerate state). This is the Egyptian Nun – the neutron soup—the origin of all matter and energy in the universe.

The movement of Sirius' companion on its own axis and around Sirius upholds all creation in space, and as such is considered the starting point of creation.

Back to the Sothic Egyptian calendar. After Julius Caesar visited to Egypt in 48 BCE, he commissioned the astronomer Sosigenes (from Alexandria) to introduce a calendar into the Roman Empire. This resulted in the Julian calendar of 365 days a year and 366 days every leap year. The Roman (Julian) calendar was literally *tailored to be fit for a King*. The first day of the year was the coronation day for the Egyptian King at his end of the annual rejuvenation jubilee [see *Egyptian Mystics: Seekers of the Way*, by same author, for more information].

However, the Julian calendar did not take into account that the year is a bit longer than 365¼ days. The difference between 365.25 days and 365.25636 days, from the time of the adoption of the Julian calendar to our present time, is 13 days. Such a difference explains the 13-day variation in the annual observations of numerous Christian festivals between the Orthodox and non-Orthodox churches. The reason is that one group followed the accurate Egyptian calendar, while the other group followed the inaccurate Julian calendar.

Since the Islamic/Arab occupation of Egypt [641 CE], the Ancient Egyptian calendar became known as the "Coptic" calendar, even though it was developed thousands of years before Christianity. Modern-day Egyptians still follow the Ancient Egyptian calendar for practically all the countless annual festivals, agriculture, weather, and other matters (with just a handful of exceptions). It is by far the most practical and accurate calendar in use in the world.

PART V : FROM MORTALS
TO IMMORTALS

Chapter 20 : Our Earthly Voyage

20.1 OUR PURPOSE ON EARTH

Mankind is always trying to understand its own reason for existence relative to the universe in which it finds itself placed.

According to the Ancient Egyptian teachings, though all creation is spiritual in origin, man is born mortal but contains within himself the seed of the divine. His purpose in this life is to nourish that seed, and his reward, if successful, is eternal life, where he will reunite with his divine origin. The ultimate objective of earthly man is to develop his/her consciousness to the utmost perfection; it means that he/she becomes harmoniously tuned with nature.

Man comes into the world with higher divine faculties, which are the essence of his/her salvation, in an unawakened state. The Egyptian teachings' aim was/is, therefore, a system of practices aimed at awakening the dormant higher faculties.

Our earthly existence is basically in a state of coma; i.e., in a state of complete unawareness. People think they're awake and aware, but they aren't. We need to bring ourselves out of the coma. This is how our souls and spirits and life essence are able to pass from this world into the more evolved states of creation towards divine union.

20.2 FROM MORTAL TO IMMORTAL

From the earliest period of Ancient Egyptian history, the Egyptians believed that Osiris was of divine origin: partly divine and partly human, who had raised himself from the dead without having seen corruption. What Osiris had effected for himself, he could effect for man.

As a model, the Ancient Egyptians believed that what Osiris did, they could do. Because he had conquered death, the righteous too might conquer death and attain everlasting life and would rise again.

Osiris represents the mortal man carrying within himself the capacity and power of spiritual salvation. Every Egyptian's hope was/is resurrection in a transformed body and immortality, which could only be realized through the death and resurrection of Osiris within each person.

The British Egyptologist, Sir E.A. Wallis Budge, summed it up on page vii of his book, *Osiris and the Egyptian Resurrection, Vol. I*, as follows:

> *"The central figure of the ancient Egyptian religion was Osiris, and the belief in his divinity, death, resurrection, and absolute control of the destinies of the bodies and souls of men. The central point of each Egyptian was his hope of resurrection in a transformed body and of immortality, which could only be realized by him through the death and resurrection of Osiris."*

Egyptian religion was an inclusive religion where Osiris lived within each of us, which facilitated a true understanding of who we are and who we are intended to become.

The principle that makes life come from apparent death was/is called Osiris, who symbolizes the power of renewal. Osiris represents the process, growth, and the underlying cyclical aspects of the universe.

The theme in the *Egyptian Book of the Caverns* talks about the necessity for death and dissolution (of the carnal and material) prior to the birth of the spiritual.

20.3 GO YOUR OWN WAY (MA-AT)

We come to earthly existence at various stages of spiritual development/progression.

One must live his/her own life, and each one of us must go his/her own way, guided by Ma-at. The concept of Ma-at has permeated all Egyptian writings from the earliest times and throughout Egyptian history. It's the concept by which not only men but also the neteru (gods, goddesses) themselves were governed. Ma-at is not easily translated or defined by one word. Basically, we might say that it means that which, of right, should be – that which is according to the proper order and harmony of the cosmos and of neteru and men, who are part of it.

Ma-at could be favorably compared with the Eastern concept of karma and the Western concept of *common sense*.

Ma-at, The Way, encompasses the virtues, goals, and duties that define acceptable, if not ideal, social interaction and personal behavior. Ma-at is maintained in the world by the correct actions and personal piety of its adherents.

Ancient Egyptian wisdom has always laid great emphasis on the cultivation of ethical behavior and service to society. The constant theme of the Egyptian wisdom literature was the 'acting out' of Truth—MaaKheru—on Earth.

A summary of the Egyptian concept of righteousness can be found in what is popularly known as the Negative Confessions [as discussed later, in the next chapter]. A more detailed picture of a righteous man and the expected conduct and the ideas of responsibility and retribution can be obtained from the walls of tomb chapels and in several literary compositions that are usually termed as wisdom texts of systematic instructions, composed of maxims and precepts. Among them are the 30 chapters of the Teaching of Amenemope (Amenhotep III), which contain many wisdom texts that were later adopted in the Old Testament's Book of Proverbs.

Numerous verbal parallels occur between this Egyptian text and the Bible, such as the opening lines of the first chapter:

> *Give your ears, listen to the words that are spoken, give your mind to interpreting them. It is profitable to put them in your heart.*

There were additional practical wisdom texts of systematic instructions composed of maxims and precepts that highlighted the Do's and Don'ts. One learns to both negate (refrain) vices and affirm (cultivate) virtues.

The Egyptian teachings emphasize that individuals must be active participants in the society, and to apply what they learn by serving others. The individual's performance in the society is the true test of his/her success.

All individuals must have productive work to support themselves and their dependents. There is no retirement from the world; i.e., no monks or hermits. The Egyptian model emphasizes a balance between living in the world and seeking spiritual experiences.

[For more detailed information, read *Egyptian Mystics: Seekers of The Way* by same author.]

20.4 PRACTICE MAKES PERFECT

The Ancient Egyptian transformational (funerary) texts are permeated with purity as a prerequisite for advancing to higher realms/heavens. The Egyptian model of mysticism stresses that purity can only be achieved through purifying the heart and practicing pure intent in ordinary daily life.

Moral behavior, for example, does not come about from merely learning certain values, but is gained through both the mind and acquired experience. Inner purification must be completed by practicing good social behavior in ordinary daily life. Every action impresses itself upon the heart.

The inward being of a person is really the reflection of his deeds and actions. Doing good deeds thus establishes good inner qualities. The virtues impressed upon the heart, in turn, govern the actions of the limbs. As each act, thought, and deed makes an image on the heart, it becomes an attribute of the person. This maturation of the soul through acquired attributes leads to progressive mystical visions and ultimate unification with the Divine.

Ancient Egyptian wisdom has always laid great emphasis on the cultivation of ethical behavior and service to society.

Progression along the spiritual Path is acquired through striving, and is a matter of conscious, disciplined action. Each new/raised consciousness is equivalent to a new awakening. The levels of consciousness are referred to as death/rebirth. Such thinking has pervaded Ancient (and present-day) Egypt, where birth and rebirth are a constant theme. The word 'death' is employed in a figurative sense. The theme that man must "die before he dies" or that he must be "born again" in his present life is taken symbolically, or is commemorated by a ritual. In this, the candidate has to pass through certain specific experiences (technically termed "deaths"). A good example is baptism, which was the main objective at Easter, after Lent, representing death of the old self by immersing into water, and the rising of the new/renewed self by coming out of the water.

20.5 THE ADVANCED ALCHEMICHAL ADVANTAGE—GOLDEN GOAL—SUFISM

Some of the Baladi Egyptians dedicate themselves to further

spiritual enlightenment. These mystics of Egypt are called "Sufis" by others. Just like their ancestors, present day Egyptian mystics dislike being given any inclusive name that might force them into doctrinal conformity. Egyptian mysticism's (and likewise, Sufism's) main keynote is the union—the identification of God and man.

A Seeker of the Way is anyone who believes that it is possible to have a direct experience of God, and who seeks such a Path. The Egyptian model of mysticism is a natural expression of personal religion in relation to the expression of religion as a communal matter. It is an assertion of a person's right to seek contact with the source of being and reality, as opposed to institutionalized religion which is based on authority and a one-way Master/slave relationship emphasizing ritual observance and legalistic morality.

Egyptian mysticism (now known as "Sufism") is (now) a name without reality. It once was a reality without a name. We only use the terms 'mystics' or 'Sufis', here, to identify them to the readers.

The Egyptian model of mysticism is not about the outer world, nor a community of believers, dogma, scriptures, rules, or rituals. It is not simply believing that God is this, or God is that, or that. It is not just asking one to "believe" and one is then automatically in God's graces. The Egyptian model of mysticism consists of ideas and practices that provide the tools for any spiritual seeker to progress along each's alchemical Path towards "union with the Divine"

The members of a fellowship are at various stages of development/progression. Those members who are more advanced, act as guides/coaches for others. There is not a clear line of distinction between clergy and laity, like there is in Christendom. Each member is learning, and at the same time is passing on his knowledge to a newer member.

20.6 THE GOLDEN GOAL—ALCHEMY

Alchemy signifies the method/power/process of transmutation of one thing into something better—symbolically, lead into gold.

Gold in true alchemy is a metaphor for ultimate spiritual accomplishment. The genuine alchemist was not practicing a misguided form of chemistry, as modern scientists like to believe: he was engaged in a spiritual quest to transform gross matter (lead) into a vehicle for the spirit (gold).

This alchemist/Sufi tradition—of transforming matter into gold – is of an Ancient Egyptian origin, as reflected in their language as follows:

– Chaotic matter in the Egyptian language is called **Ben,** which has several related meanings: *the primordial stone, the mound of creation, the first state of matter, opposition/ negation, it is not, there is not, and multiplicity.*

– The mirror image of **Ben** is **Neb** (Ben spelled backwards), which also has several related meanings: *gold* (traditionally, the finished, perfected end product—the goal of the alchemist), *lord, master, all, affirmation, and pure.*

Thoth, the Ancient Egyptian neter (god), is recognized by all early (and later) Sufi writers as the ancient model of alchemy, mysticism, and all related subjects. The well-known Sufi writer Idries Shah admits the role of Egypt via Thoth and Dhu'I-Nun on Sufism and alchemy as follows:

> *"... alchemical lore came from Egypt direct from the writings of Thoth*
>
> *... According to Sufi tradition the lore was transmitted through Dhu'i-Nun the Egyptian, the King or Lord of the Fish, one of the most famous of classical Sufi teachers. [The Sufis, 1964]*

Thoth's name appears among the ancient masters of what is now called the *Way of the Sufis*. In other words: both the Sufis and the alchemists recognize Thoth as the foundation of their knowledge.

Idries Shah also makes a direct reference to the Spanish Arab historian Said of Toledo (died in 1069), who gives this tradition of the Ancient Egyptian Thoth:

> **"Sages affirm that all antediluvian sciences originate with the Egyptian Hermes [Thoth], in Upper Egypt (namely Khmunu (Hermopolis)). The Jews call him Enoch and the Moslems Idris. He was the first who spoke of the material of the superior world and of planetary movements . . . Medicine and poetry were his functions . . . [as well as] the sciences, including alchemy and magic.** [Cf. Asin Palacios, Ibn Masarra, p. 13] Masarra means Egyptian

Egyptian mysticism encompasses basically two types of spiritual experience:

1. A quest for spiritual self-development in the form of ethical self-control and worldly personal religious insight. The aspirant who is able to purify himself is ready now for the second quest.
2. The quest to find God in the manifested world as well as finding the manifested world in God. This is accomplished through gaining knowledge by using both intellect and intuition in order to transcend the limitations of our human senses.

[More detailed information about this subject in *Egyptian Mystics: Seekers of The Way* by same author.]

Chapter 21 : Climbing The Heavenly Ladder—Life After Earth

21.1 THE SOUL TRANSMIGRATION

The Egyptians' preoccupation—almost obsession— with the ideas of birth and rebirth was a fundamental element of their funerary beliefs: rebirth was one of the stages of existence in the afterlife. Egyptian texts state clearly that *the soul is in heaven, the body in the earth*" [Pepi I Tomb]; i.e., they never expected the physical body to rise again.

The first known reference to a "second birth" occurs in the CLXXXII[nd] Chapter of *The Book of Coming Forth by Light*, wherein Osiris is addressed as:

> *...he [Osiris] who giveth birth to men and women a second time.*

"The Egyptians", according to Herodotus, *"were the first to maintain that the soul of man is immortal".* The doctrine of transmigration is also mentioned by Plutarch, Plato, and other ancient writers as being the general belief among the Egyptians, and it was adopted by Pythagoras and his preceptor Pherecydes, as well as other philosophers of Greece.

21.2 PERFORMANCE EVALUATION

In a book of instructions, an Egyptian King advised his son, the prince, to attain the highest qualities because upon his death, he would see his whole lifetime in a single instant, and his performance on earth would be reviewed and evaluated by the judges. Even as far back as the period of the 6th Dynasty we find the idea that heaven was reserved for those who had performed their duty to man and to the Divine Powers while on earth. No exceptions were made for a King or anyone else.

For example, the Pharaoh Unas (2323 BCE), before he was ready to fly from earth into heaven, was not allowed to start unless the neteru (who were about to help him) were satisfied as to the reality of his moral worth. They demanded that no man should have uttered a word against him on Earth, and that no complaint should have been made against him in heaven before the neteru (gods). Accordingly, in the text of Unas, we read:

> **Unas hath not been spoken against on earth before men,**
> **he hath not been accused of sin in heaven before the neteru**
> (gods, goddesses).

As stated earlier, the Ancient Egyptians expressed their metaphysical beliefs in a story form, like a sacred drama or a mystery play. The following are the Egyptians' symbolic representations of the process of the Judgment Day Mystery Play:

1. The soul of the deceased is led to the Hall of Judgment of the Double-Ma-at. She is double because the scale balances only when there is an equality of opposing forces. Ma-at's symbol is the ostrich feather, representing judgment or truth. Her feather is customarily mounted on the scales.

2. Anubis, as opener of the way, guides the deceased to the scales and weighs the heart.

1. Ma-at, 2. Anubis, 3. Amam (Ammit), 4. Thoth,

5. The deceased, 6. Horus, 7. Osiris, 8. 42 Judges/Assessors

The heart, as a metaphor for conscience, is weighed against the feather of truth, to determine the fate of the deceased.

3. The seated Osiris presides in the Hall of Justice. The jury consists of 42 judges/assessors. Each judge has a specific jurisdiction over a specific sin or fault. Each wears a feather of truth on his/her head.

4. The spirit of the deceased denies committing each sin/fault before its assigned judge, by reciting the 42 Negative Confessions. These Negative Confessions come from Chapter CXXV of *The Book of the Coming Forth by Light* (commonly known as *The Book of the Dead*).

The assigned juror/judge will declare his/her acceptance by declaring ***Maa-Kheru*** (True of Voice/Action).

Here is a translation of the 42 Negative Confessions. Some of them may seem repetitive, but this is caused by the inability to translate the exact intent and meaning of the original language.

1. I have not done iniquity.

2. *I have not robbed with violence.*

3. *I have not stolen.*

4. *I have done no murder; I have done no harm.*

5. *I have not defrauded offerings.*

6. *I have not diminished obligations.*

7. *I have not plundered the neteru.*

8. *I have not spoken lies.*

9. *I have not uttered evil words.*

10. *I have not caused pain.*

11. *I have not committed fornication.*

12. *I have not caused shedding of tears.*

13. *I have not dealt deceitfully.*

14. *I have not transgressed.*

15. *I have not acted guilefully.*

16. *I have not laid waste the ploughed land.*

17. *I have not been an eavesdropper.*

18. *I have not set my lips in motion (against any man).*

19. *I have not been angry and wrathful except for a just cause.*

20. *I have not defiled the wife of any man.*

21. *I have not been a man of anger.*

22. *I have not polluted myself.*

23. *I have not caused terror.*

24. *I have not burned with rage.*

25. *I have not stopped my ears against the words of Right and Truth. (Ma-at)*

26. *I have not worked grief.*

27. *I have not acted with insolence.*

28. *I have not stirred up strife.*

29. *I have not judged hastily.*

30. *I have not sought for distinctions.*

31. *I have not multiplied words exceedingly.*

32. *I have not done neither harm nor ill.*

33. *I have not cursed the King. (i.e. violation of laws)*

34. *I have not fouled the water.*

35. I have not spoken scornfully.

36. I have never cursed the neteru.

37. I have not stolen.

38. I have not defrauded the offerings of the neteru.

39. I have not plundered the offerings of the blessed dead.

40. I have not filched the food of the infant.

41. I have not sinned against the neter of my native town.

42. I have not slaughtered with evil intent the cattle of the neter.

5. Thoth, scribe of the neteru (gods, goddesses), records the verdict as Anubis weighs the heart against the feather of truth. The outcome is either:

a. If the pans are not balanced, this means that this person lived simply as matter. As a result, Amam (Ammit) would eat this heart. Amam is a protean crossbreed.

The unperfected soul will be reborn again (reincarnated) in a new physical vehicle (body), in order to provide the soul an opportunity for further development on earth. This cycle of life/death/renewal continues until the soul is perfected, by fulfilling the 42 Negative Confessions, during his life on earth.

b. If the two pans are perfectly balanced, Osiris gives favorable judgment, and gives his final **Maa-Kheru** (True of Voice).

The perfected soul will go through the process of transformation and subsequent rebirth. The outcome of his/her evaluation will determine which heavenly level (2-6) a person reaches.

21.3 TRANSFORMATIONAL TEXTS

The object of one and all Ancient Egyptian transformational

(funerary) texts was the same, namely, to procure the resurrection and immortality of the persons on whose behalf they were written and recited. Accompanying texts to the deceased varied in content and style. No transformational ("funerary") texts of any two persons were ever the same. These texts were tailored to match each individual's path. We find the same individuality of texts in the so-called "magical" papyri. The Egyptian texts described in detail the stages of the transformation process from man's earthly existence to the different metaphysical realms.

All these themes are treated with a profusion of details in *The Book of Coming Forth By Light* (Per-em-hru), wrongly translated and commonly known as *The Egyptian Book of the Dead*. It consists of over one hundred chapters of varying lengths, which are closely related to the Unas Transformational (Funerary) Texts at Saqqara. This book is to be found, in its complete form, only on papyrus scrolls that were wrapped in the mummy swathing of the deceased and buried with him.

Other transformational (so-called funerary and religious) writings are also closely related to the above-mentioned Unas Transformational Funerary (Pyramid) Texts. Each text/writing explores the same basic theme of life/death/rebirth – i.e., the transformation of the soul in the region of the Duat after death – from a different angle. Since no two persons are alike, no two transformational texts are alike. These compositions are known as: *The Book of What Is In the Duat* (or Underworld), *The Book of the Gates*, *The Book of Caverns*, *The Litany of Ra*, *The Book of Aker*, *The Book of Day*, and *The Book of Night*.

21.4 ADMISSION TO THE NEW REALM

As a result of the performance evaluation, the departed spirits go to various realms depending on each's achievement level during their earthly existence.

The transformational texts set in motion the process by which the new soul progresses from one realm to another. S/he must meet other requirements and be accepted before proceeding further. To be admitted to a new realm, the dwellers of each realm must find the newcomer qualified and worthy of joining or passing through that realm. The tenants' rights in the spirited world are the same as in the earthly realm. [See details in an earlier chapter of this book.]

The newcomer needs both acceptance and assistance of each realm-dweller as s/he ascends higher and higher. So, in the Unas tomb (rubble pyramid) at Saqqara, we find that the inhabitants of the higher realms—The People of Light—found Unas (~2323 BCE) to be worthy, and thus are accepting and helping him to ascend and to live among them:

Utterance 336

The People of Light bore witness for him;
the hail showers of the sky took hold of him.
They let Unas ascend to Re.

Utterance 377

Your smell comes to Unas, ye neteru (gods, goddesses),
the smell of Unas comes to you, ye neteru.
May Unas be with you, ye neteru,
may you be together with Unas, ye neteru.
May Unas live with you, ye neteru,
may you live together with Unas, ye neteru

21.5 THE GLORY

In the Ancient Egyptian texts, the realized soul achieves glory and joins the Divine Origin.

After a long series of adventurous journeys, the resurrected soul, justified and regenerated, will attain a place in the retinue of the neteru (gods, goddesses)—the cosmic forces—and eventually take part in the unceasing round of activity that permits the universe a continued existence. The Egyptian writing describes that it:

> *becomes a star of gold and joins the company of Re, and sails with him across the sky in his boat of millions of years.*

Glory is the radiant beauty of splendor and magnificence—heaven or the bliss of heaven—which is attained by the highest achievement. Glory is represented in artwork as a halo or a circle of light. In Ancient Egypt, the neter (god) Re represents the Light and is depicted as a circle.

The relationship between the cycle of death and resurrection is reflected in the Egyptian form of the "name"of Osiris being **Ausar**, which consists of two syllables—**Aus-Ra**. The first syllable of the name (Aus-Ra) is pronounced *Aus* or *Os*, meaning "strength, might, power". The name of the **neter** (god) means something like the *strength of Re*. This meaning describes the true essence of the neter (god) Osiris.

In the cycle of **Aus-Ra**, **Ausar** (Osiris) is identified with the moon, the light of the night regions of the dead. **Ausar's** Light is a reflection of **Ra** (Re), in one of his manifestations as the sun.

Ausar died (analogous to the moon's departure, near the end of the lunar month) and was resurrected the third day after that. The third day is the beginning of a new moon, i.e. a renewed **Ausar**. This is reminiscent of the Easter celebration where, like **Ausar**, the biblical Jesus died on Friday and was resurrected the third day (Sunday) as a new life.

Ausar (Osiris) is written in hieroglyphs with the glyph of the throne and the eye, combining the concepts of legitimacy and divinity.

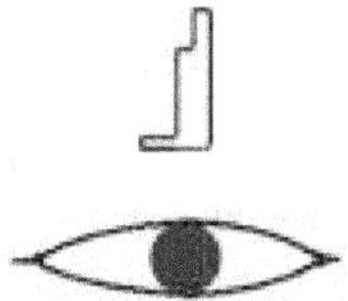

Ra (Re) is associated with the glyph of the eye. The most distinctive Egyptian symbol is the eye, which plays many complex and subtle roles. The eye is the part of the body able to perceive the light, and is therefore a symbol for spiritual ability.

Ra (Re) is the cosmic principle of energy that moves toward death, and **Ausar** (Osiris) represents the process of rebirth. Thus, the terms of life and death become interchangeable: life means slow dying; death means resurrection to new life. The dead person in death is identified with **Ausar**, but he will come to life again, and will be identified with **Ra**.

SELECTED BIBLIOGRAPHY

Assmann, J. *Agyptische Hymnen Und Gebete* (Leiden Papyrus p. 312-321). Zürich/Münich, 1975.

Breasted, James Henry. *Ancient Records of Egypt*, 3 Vols. Chicago, USA, 1927.

Budge, E.A. Wallis. *Amulets and Superstitions*. New York, 1978.

Budge, E.A. Wallis. *Egyptian Religion: Egyptian Ideas of the Future Life*. London, 1975.

Budge, E.A. Wallis. *From Fetish to God in Ancient Egypt*. London, 1934.

Budge, E.A. Wallis. *The Gods of the Egyptians*, 2 volumes. New York, 1969.

Budge, Wallis. *Osiris & The Egyptian Resurrection* (2 volumes). New York, 1973.

Clement Stromata Book V, chapter IV [www.piney.com/Clement-Stromata-Five.html]

Diodorus of Sicily. *Books I, II, & IV*, tr. By C.H. Oldfather. London, 1964

Egyptian Book of the Dead (The Book of Going Forth by Day), The Papyrus of Ani. USA, 1991.

Erman, Adolf. *Life in Ancient Egypt*. New York, 1971.

Farouk Ahmed Moustafa. *The Mouleds: A Study in the Popular Customs and Traditions in Egypt*. Alexandria, 1981 [Arabic text].

Gadalla, Moustafa:
- *Ancient Egyptian Culture Revealed*. USA, 2007.
- *Egyptian Cosmology: The Animated Universe—2nd edition*. USA, 2001.
- *Egyptian Divinities: The All Who Are THE ONE*. USA, 2001.
- *Egyptian Harmony: The Visual Music*. USA, 2000.
- *Egyptian Mystics: Seekers of the Way*. USA, 2003.
- *The Ancient Egyptian Roots of Christianity*. USA, 2007.
- *Egyptian Rhythm: The Heavenly Melodies*. USA, 2002.
- *Egyptian Romany: The Essence of Hispania*. USA, 2004.
- *Historical Deception: The Untold Story of Ancient Egypt*. USA, 1999.

Gilsenan, Michael. *Saint and Sufi in Modern Egypt*. Oxford, 1973.

Horapollo. *The Hieroglyphics of Horapollo*. Tr. By George Boas, New York, 1950.

Herodotus. *The Histories*, tr. A. de Selincourt. New York and Harmondsworth, 1954.

James, T.G.H. *An Introduction to Ancient Egypt*. London, 1979.

Kastor, Joseph. *Wings of the Falcon, Life and Thought of Ancient Egypt*. USA, 1968.

Kepler, Johannes. *The Harmony of the World*. Tr. by E. J. Aiton. USA, 1997.

Khaldûn, Ibn. *The Muqaddimah: An Introduction to History*, tr. From the Arabic by Franz Rosenthal, abridged and edited by N.J. Dawood. Princeton, 1969.

Lambelet, Edouard. *Gods and Goddesses in Ancient Egypt*. Cairo, 1986.

Lane, E.W. *The Manners and Customs of the Modern Egyptians*. London, 1836.

Parkinson, R.B. *Voices From Ancient Egypt, An Anthology of Middle Kingdom Writings*. London, 1991.

Peet, T. Eric. *The Rhind Mathematical Papyrus*. London, 1923.

Piankoff, Alexandre. *The Litany of Re*. New York, 1964.

Piankoff, Alexandre. *Mythological Papyri*. New York, 1957.

Piankoff, Alexandre. *The Pyramid of Unas Texts*. Princeton, NJ, USA, 1968.

Piankoff, Alexandre. *The Shrines of Tut-Ankh-Amon Texts*. New York, 1955.

Piankoff, Alexandre. *The Tomb of Ramesses VI*. New York, 1954.

Plato. *The Collected Dialogues of Plato including the Letters*. Edited by E. Hamilton & H. Cairns. New York, 1961.

Plotinus. *The Enneads*, in 6 volumes, Tr. By A.H. Armstrong. London, 1978.

Plotinus. *The Enneads*, Tr. By Stephen MacKenna. London, 1991.

Plutarch. *De Iside Et Osiride*. Tr. By J. Gwyn Griffiths. Wales, U.K., 1970.

Plutarch. *Plutarch's Moralia, Volume V*. Tr. by Frank Cole Babbitt. London, 1927.

Siculus, Diodorus. *Vol 1*. Tr. by C.H. Oldfather. London.

Silverman, David and Torode, Brian. *The Material Word: Some Theories of Language and its Limits*. London, 1980.

West, John A. *The Travelers Key to Ancient Egypt*. New York, 1989.

Wilkinson, Richard H. *Reading Egyptian Art*. New York, 1994.

Wilkinson, Sir J. Gardner. *The Ancient Egyptians, Their Life and Customs*. London, 1988.

————. *Wings of the Falcon, Life and Thought of Ancient Egypt*, tr. Joseph Kaster. USA, 1968.

Numerous references written in Arabic.

Several Internet sources.

2

SOURCES AND NOTES

References to sources in the previous section, Selected Bibliography are only referred to for facts, events, and dates—not for their interpretations of such information.

The absence of several references in the Selected Bibliography does not mean that the author is unfamiliar with them. It only means that in spite of their "popularity", they were not found to be credible sources.

It should be noted that if a reference is made to one of author Moustafa Gadalla's books, each of his books contains appendices for its own extensive bibliography as well as detailed Sources and Notes.

Chapter 1: The Most Religious

The Egyptians' Cosmic Consciousness—All references, even if most references call it "superstition", which still means cosmic consciousness.

The Unity of Multiplicity of the Universe—Budge (all), West, Piankoff (Re), Kaster. Gadalla (Cosmology 2nd ed., Divinities)

Amen-Renef: The Undefined—Budge (all), West, Piankoff (all), Kaster, Gadalla (Cosmology 2nd ed., Divinities)

Chapter 2: The Animating Energies of The Universe

Practically all references, Budge (all), West, Piankoff (all), Kaster, Plutarch, Gadalla (Cosmology 2nd ed., Divinities & Romany), Gadalla (being a native Egyptian), numerous books in Arabic.

Chapter 3: The Pictorial Metaphysical Images

Silverman, (Ibn) Khadun, West, Gadalla (Cosmology 2nd ed., Divinities, Rhythm & Harmony), Plutarch, Piankoff (Re), Horapollo, Budge.

Chapter 4: The Egyptian Creation Process Accounts

Practically all references, Assmann. Budge (all), West, Piankoff (Re), Kaster, Gadalla (Cosmology 2nd ed., Divinities & Romany)

Chapter 5: Numerology of the Creation Process

Assmann, Plutarch, Plotinus, West, Gadalla (Cosmology 2nd ed. & Harmony)

Chapter 6: The Dualistic Nature

Piankoff (all references), Budge, West, Kaster, Plotinus, Lambelet, Gadalla (Egyptian Cosmology 2nd ed., Harmony, Christianity, Mystics), Book of Coming Forth By Light, Papyrus of Ani, Gadalla (being an Egyptian native), and numerous books in Arabic.

Chapter 7: Three—Trinities

Assmann, Piankoff (all references), Plutarch, Diodorus, Budge, West, Kaster, Gadalla (Egyptian Cosmology 2nd ed.,

Harmony, Christianity, Mystics), Book of Coming Forth By Light, Papyrus of Ani.

Chapter 8: The Stability of Four

Practically all references. Gadalla (Egyptian Cosmology 2nd ed., Mystics).
Four Elements – Plutarch.
Leiden Papyrus – Assmann.
Tet Pillar – Budge.

Chapter 9: The Fifth Star

Plutarch, Assmann, Budge, Gadalla (Egyptian Cosmology 2nd ed., Egyptian Harmony).

Chapter 10: The Cubical Six

Gadalla (Egyptian Cosmology 2nd ed., Harmony, Mystics), West.

Chapter 11: The Cyclical Seven

Budge, Piankoff (all references), Gadalla (Egyptian Cosmology 2nd ed., Divinities).

Chapter 12: Eight, The Octave

Assmann, Parkinson (Coffin Texts), Gadalla (Egyptian Cosmology 2nd ed., Divinities), Kaster, Erman

Chapter 13: Nine Lives

Budge, Assmann, Kaster, Piankoff, Gadalla (Egyptian Cosmology 2nd ed., Divinities), Book of Coming Forth By Light, Papyrus of Ani.

Chapter 14: Ten, a New One

Budge, Assmann, Kaster, Piankoff, Gadalla (Egyptian Cosmology 2nd ed., Divinities).

Chapter 15: The Human Being—The Universal Replica

Budge, Painkoff (Re, Unas), Papyrus of Ani, Kaster, Wilkinson,R. H., Gadalla (Egyptian Cosmology, 2nd ed., Harmony), West

Chapter 16: Social & Political System

Herodotus, Diodorus, Gadalla (Cosmology 2nd ed., Culture), Budge, Plutarch, Book of Coming Forth By Light, Papyrus of Ani, Gadalla being a native Egyptian.

Chapter 17: The Cosmic Link

Diodorus, Gadalla (Cosmology 2nd ed., Culture), Budge, Plutarch, West, Book of Coming Forth By Light, Papyrus of Ani, Gadalla being a native Egyptian.

Chapter 18: The Physical/Metaphysical Society

Gadalla (Cosmology 2nd ed., Culture, Mystics), Budge, Plutarch, Book of Coming Forth By Light, Papyrus of Ani, Gadalla being a native Egyptian.

Chapter 19: Astronomical Consciousness

Clement, Gadalla (Cosmology, 2nd ed., Rhythm, Mystics), Budge, West, Wilkinson, Kepler, Parkinson [re: the astronomical record-keeping of Sabt (Sirius) Star], Gadalla being a native Egyptian.

Chapter 20: Our Earthly Voyage

Kaster, Gadalla (Christianity, Cosmology, 2nd ed., Mystics), Budge, Piankoff, practically all references.

Chapter 21: Climbing The Heavenly Ladder

Herodotus, Budge, Book of Coming Forth By Light, Papyrus of Ani, Piankoff (Unas, Mythological Papyri), Gadalla (Cosmology 2nd ed., Mystics, Christianity), West, practically all references.

Appendix 1: Isis and Osiris allegory

Gadalla (Christianity), Budge, Plutarch, practically all references.